CINESCOPES

"★★★★!"

D0973159

CINESCOPES

"★★★★!"

WHAT YOUR FAVORITE MOVIES REVEAL ABOUT YOU

by Risa Williams and Ezra Werb

QUIRK BOOKS

PHILADELPHIA

We dedicate this book to movie lovers everywhere.

★ ★ ★ ★

Library of Congress Cataloging in Publication Number: 2007932764

ISBN: 978-1-59474-191-3

Printed in China

Typeset in Goudy Sans and Helvetica Compressed

Designed by Karen Onorato
Illustrations by Sylvia Kay

Distributed in North America by Chronicle Books
680 Second Street
San Francisco, CA 94107

10 9 8 7 6 5 4 3 2 1

Quirk Books
215 Church Street
Philadelphia, PA 19106
www.quirkbooks.com

Contents ★★★★★★★★★★★★★★★★★★★★★★★★★★★★★

INTRODUCTION

Discovering something new about your personality is as easy as making a list of your ten favorite movies. *Cinescopes* is a unique personality assessment system based on heroic archetypes commonly found in movies. We've identified sixteen different personality types that describe the core character makeup of every movie fan. By matching a list of your ten favorite films to our extensive film glossary, you can unlock your personal Cinescope and discover a little more about what makes you tick.

Since the very beginning, humans have been drawn to stories about heroic journeys, because in watching a hero conquer an obstacle, we learn something about ourselves. Joseph Campbell, a writer and expert on mythology, once said: "The myth . . . gives you a line to connect with that mystery which you are."

Movies are the mythic tales of today. They can make us cry, scream, or laugh. They can cheer us up or bring us down. And just like those ancient stories of humans struggling for the favor of the gods, movies tend to focus on a hero undertaking some kind of journey, whether it be physical, intellectual, or emotional.

We all enjoy watching a hero struggle against an obstacle, but there are truths we can learn about ourselves as individuals based on the kinds of heroes we appreciate most. Some people are moved by Debra Winger's character facing cancer in *Terms of Endearment*, while others prefer to watch Arnold Schwarzenegger gunning people down in *The Terminator*. These very different heroes communicate different messages about life, and that's the idea that sparked our book.

We compared the personality characteristics of hundreds of movie fans against their list of favorite movies to develop our sixteen Cinescope types. In turn, we've learned that if you like to watch swashbuckling adventurers, then you're probably a cultured individual whose boldness is respected by colleagues. If you like to watch Rebellious Lovers having steamy onscreen affairs, you're probably an open-minded individual who fantasizes about true love. We can even predict that if you like movies featuring Invincible Optimists, then you probably bring cupcakes to work and you're in constant social demand.

In the pages that follow, you can discover more about how the movies you watch can reveal aspects of your innermost personality. Your taste in movies can even speak to the relationships you'll have with other movie fans—which Cinescope types are your best matches, and which are your worst. You'll even learn more about the personality of your ultimate nemesis, that person who seems to calculate every move to prevent you from being happy, whether it's by stealing your stapler, hitting on your date, or complaining endlessly at your birthday party.

Can all this possibly be true? Can your favorite movies really reveal so much about your personality? See for yourself! After reading our book, perhaps you'll look at yourself in a whole new light. Or perhaps you'll just get a kick out of discovering what types of stories you're drawn to. But one thing is certain—once you look through the lens of *Cinescopes*, movies will never seem the same again.

HOW TO
USE THIS BOOK

Visit our Web site, **www.cinescopes.com**, and fill in your ten favorite movies. You will instantly receive the name and code of your Cinescopes personality type. Match your code to the corresponding Cinescope in this book. Or

1. Make a list of your ten favorite movies.
2. Look up your favorite movie titles in the glossary beginning on page 139, and write down the Cinescope codes that appear next to each. In some cases, a movie title will have more than one code; write down all the codes associated with each title.
3. Look at all the codes to see which appears most often.
4. Match that code to the corresponding Cinescope in this book (see The Movie Glossary Legend on page 140). In the case of a tie, read both Cinescopes and decide for yourself which best describes your personality.
5. Repeat the process with everyone you know!

"I CAN'T THINK OF TEN FAVORITE MOVIES!"

Here are some questions to help you focus. And remember—you can always adjust your list if you think of something better later on.

What movies do you own a copy of? ★ What movie have you seen so many times you can recite the dialogue? ★ What movie made you laugh so hard it hurt? ★ What movie made you cry uncontrollably? ★ What movie made you so afraid you couldn't be alone in the dark? ★ What movie made you applaud at the end? ★ What movies are you embarrassed to love? ★ What movie can you watch every time it's on TV?

CHARISMATIC PERFORMER

Glossary Code: CP

All the world's a stage, and the men and women merely players. No one knows this better than Charismatic Performers. Artistic, talented, and witty, these heroes are natural charmers who win everyone, even the most resistant, over. Somehow, it's easier for them to hide their fears in the spotlight than in the shadows. Ultimately, no one knows who they really are, but once these heroes trust someone enough to reveal their true colors, they will release their deepest fears forever.

Performers appreciate the finer things in life: an aged wine, a well-prepared meal, an artfully decorated apartment. They enjoy the form and style of things, appreciate aesthetics and architecture, and are witty, gifted, and clever. As Margo says in *All About Eve*, when a Charismatic Performer is around, "It's going to be a bumpy night!"

Famous Charismatic Performers

- ★ Wolfgang Amadeus Mozart in *Amadeus*
- ★ Fanny Brice in *Funny Girl*
- ★ Don Lockwood in *Singin' in the Rain*
- ★ Margo Channing in *All About Eve*
- ★ Norma Desmond in *Sunset Blvd.*
- ★ Ray Charles in *Ray*

Charismatic Performer Typecasting

- ★ Gene Kelly
- ★ Judy Garland
- ★ Marilyn Monroe
- ★ Frank Sinatra
- ★ Rupert Everett
- ★ Barbra Streisand

Personality Strengths ★★★★★★★★★★★★★★★★★★★★★★★★★★

Performers are loaded with all sorts of talent. Even if they're not trained thespians, they certainly know how to *act*. They might be able to read tea leaves, play cards well, or cook like a chef. They've got heaps of charm and cultural knowledge that they use to dazzle fans.

Performers are great at improvising their way out of bad situations. They can talk their way out of speeding tickets and return expensive electronics even when they're responsible for the damage. They've got a boisterous laugh, and they know how to use it. A serious argument with a friend will quickly subside with a few chuckles, eventually turning into a nice shared memory: "Remember when I almost punched you in the face? Ah, good times."

Performers are deft at sizing people up. They can give on-the-spot, accurate psychoanalyses based on the person's hairstyle and shoes. They're perceptive and clever about human behavior. They'll pick up on the tiny social cues that the rest of us miss completely, and they always use this skill to their best advantage.

QUINTESSENTIAL STATEMENTS

"This is my happening, and it freaks me out!"—Ronnie "Z-Man" Barzell in *Beyond the Valley of the Dolls*

"To love oneself is the beginning of a lifelong romance."—Lord Arthur Goring in *An Ideal Husband*

"The only true currency in this bankrupt world . . . is what you share with someone else when you're uncool."—Lester Bangs in *Almost Famous*

"I always say a kiss on the hand might feel very good, but a diamond tiara lasts forever."—Lorelei Lee in *Gentlemen Prefer Blondes*

"Some day you won't laugh at me! I'm going out and have a real life! I'm gonna be somebody!"—Esther Blodgett in *A Star Is Born*

"I am the Lizard King . . . I can do anything!"—Jim Morrison in *The Doors*

Personality Weaknesses ★★★★★★★★★★★★★★★★★★★★★★★★

Performers are hard workers who are prone to perfectionism. They have a hard time gauging what is realistic and reasonable to accomplish; they'll be mad at themselves for not climbing Mount Kilimanjaro by the age of twenty, and they'll hate themselves because Mozart wrote *Andante* at the age of five. This constant pressure tends to make them snap easily. The inner stress that accumulates may cause them to hurl something at an assistant, toss a lover's clothes out the window, or cry hysterically when listening to Billie Holiday.

When Performers hit the wall, they retreat into themselves, grow broody, and resist socializing. In these phases, they really can't accomplish much personally or professionally.

TYPICAL MODES OF TRANSPORTATION

Tour bus ★ Carried by a mob of adoring fans ★ On a train, incognito ★ Lowered down by ropes ★ Through a trapdoor

CULINARY FAVORITES

Whatever they like, whenever they please ★ Sherry ★ Sweets from admirers ★ Champagne and caviar ★ Grapes fed by manservant ★ Something strange from somewhere exotic

Their Deepest Secret ★

On the outside, Performers seem open and uninhibited. In reality, they are just putting up a cover for the person who lives beneath the façade. They may be able to charm people with their skills, but they don't believe that their skills represent their inner selves. They crave admiration for their intellect and their hearts more than for their outward accomplishments. They secretly pine for an existence out of the spotlight, a quiet place where they can take off their costume, put down the microphone, and just be.

Charismatic Performers at Work ★ ★ ★ ★ ★ ★ ★ ★ ★ ★ ★ ★ ★ ★ ★ ★

At work, Performers are exceedingly popular and loved. However, their biggest fans may be the ones who irritate them the most: the secretary with her nasal laugh or the weird guy with Ziggy cartoons taped to his computer. Performers often wish that more refined people found them more appealing. Then again, any press is good press.

Coworkers appreciate having Performers around. Performers are social and fun—they'll gladly take everyone at work to the local sushi bar for karaoke. They're also generous; they'll pick up the tab without hesitation. They delight in making a group event more joyous.

Bosses like Performers. After all, they make the office buzz with excitement, and bosses are not immune to their charms. If Performers dislike their boss, they will fantasize daily about storming out of the job after delivering an Oscar-worthy monologue. They're very unlikely to act out such a fantasy, but they derive an impish thrill from imagining they will.

Charismatic Performers with Friends ★ ★ ★ ★ ★ ★ ★ ★ ★ ★ ★ ★ ★ ★

Friends love to go out on the town with Performers. Performers are refined and cultured, and they know how to say just the right things. Their body language and their very presence seem to set people at ease, and friends can count on Performers to enrich places with a contagious, energetic enthusiasm. Performers are also handy with a drink—in fact, they'll fill your glass before you even realize you're thirsty.

Friends tend to think of Performers as witty, charming, and a little too emotional. Although friends appreciate the fact that a Performer feels deeply about their passions, they get annoyed when a Performer gets huffy over small things like a slightly cold cup of coffee. Performers can sometimes demand too much from their friends, and their feelings are easily bruised. Friends can't always count on a Performer to contain their dissatisfaction—Performers express their feelings right away. Luckily, Performers have no problem facing conflicts, and they bury grudges easily.

QUINTESSENTIAL BEHAVIOR

Humiliating a two-timer in front of a crowd. ★ Staging a theatrical production in a barn. ★ Spontaneously singing while wading in a public fountain. ★ Getting drunk and playing a piano upside down. ★ Wearing glasses to conceal your true identity. ★ Wearing glasses and dressing up like the opposite sex just for the hell of it.

Charismatic Performers in Love ★ ★ ★ ★ ★ ★ ★ ★ ★ ★ ★ ★ ★ ★ ★ ★

Performers often attract introverts who are drawn to their confidence. Performers fall into these relationships easily and help their partners grow. However, Performers will come to crave the kind of understanding that can only be provided by someone who is like them.

When they're in love, Performers will play the part like a great romantic lead in a classic Hollywood feature. They behave suavely on the surface: breakfasts in bed, candlelit dinners, and whirlwind first dates. This is partially to impress and partially to disguise their insecurities about the future. They're often passionate in bed and expert love-makers.

In long-term relationships, Performers tend to become overly sensitive to their companions' little faults, and tensions often arise. In order for their relationships to work, Performers must learn to be vulnerable to their partners and to allow their partners to be vulnerable toward them. When they do this, they'll grow with their mate both spiritually and emotionally.

MUST-SEE MOVIES FOR
CHARISMATIC PERFORMERS

Charismatic Performers like their movies to be full of colorful sets and costumes, showcasing artists in their creative struggle. They prefer grand film spectacles that feature multitalented stars.

An American in Paris (1951)	*On the Town* (1949)	*Top Hat* (1935)
Immortal Beloved (1994)	*Pollock* (2000)	*Victor/Victoria* (1982)
Love is the Devil (1998)	*Strictly Ballroom* (1992)	*Vincent & Theo* (1990)
Man on the Moon (1999)	*Sweet and Lowdown* (1999)	*Waiting for Guffman* (1996)

Most Compatible Cinescope Types ★★★★★★★★★★★★★★

The Enlightened Healer. It's true that all performers need a stabilizing force to ground them in the realm of everyday life. Healers can play this role for Charismatic Performers, and they enjoy living vicariously through their successes and failures. In *Walk the Line*, June Carter (Healer) nurses Johnny Cash (Performer) through his alcoholism and drug abuse to keep his career and life going.

The Invincible Optimist. Optimists are funny and bright, and they know how to floor a room with a joke. Their comfort in social settings makes them good companions for Performers, who are witty and charming themselves. If the two can resist trying to outdo one another, they can take the world by storm. Like Don Lockwood (Performer) and Cosmo Brown (Optimist) in *Singin' in the Rain*, they know how to make 'em laugh.

Least Compatible Cinescope Type ★ ★ ★ ★ ★ ★ ★ ★ ★ ★ ★ ★ ★ ★ ★ ★ ★ ★

The Loyal Warrior. Although Performers truly appreciate their family and friends, they feel that Loyal Warriors take this sentiment too far. Warriors will do anything for the team, devoting themselves to the group, causing Performers to crave more individual attention from Warriors. Additionally, Performers might resent that Warriors don't see them as unique, and Warriors might resent that Performers demand special treatment. In *Boogie Nights*, Dirk Diggler (Performer) rises to stardom and leaves his surrogate father and director, Jack Horner (Warrior), in the dust.

Other Cinescope Types Who Are Hard Working ★ ★ ★ ★ ★ ★ ★ ★ ★

Like Performers, **Courageous Detectives** and **Dedicated Idealists** approach their work with unmatched determination. Detectives and Performers use their natural instinct to get ahead; Idealists and Performers take on huge risks and obstacles. Idealists and Performers can make great friends because they both have big dreams and big talent. In love, Idealists might be too practical for Performers, and Detectives might be too straightforward.

Other Cinescope Types Who Have Big Goals ★ ★ ★ ★ ★ ★ ★ ★ ★ ★

Chosen Adventurers and **Youthful Sages.** Much like Performers, Adventurers and Sages set ambitious goals that feel impossible to attain. Sages are very practical, and since Performers dread balancing their checkbooks, they'd quarrel frequently. Adventurers and Performers are both aggressive, but in completely different ways—both types love to travel and might enjoy a few globetrotting affairs together without getting too serious.

The Charismatic Performer's Greatest Nemesis ★ ★ ★ ★ ★ ★ ★ ★

The Eternal Critic. Try as they might, Eternal Critics never attain the charm and grace that Performers have mastered. As a result, Eternal Critics spend their lives exposing the flaws of the Performers. Critics never offer their support; they only offer stinging, hurtful words that pierce through the hearts of Performers. Their weakness lies in the fact that they are, essentially, powerless. Once Performers learn that words can't hurt them, Critics will find that they have lost their edge. In *All About Eve*, Addison de Witt (Critic) tears down Margo Channing (Performer) with vicious words and evil maneuvers.

Why do Performers hate Critics so much? Critics vocalize all of the doubts that Performers obsess over. Performers must eradicate their inner Critic or they may start to unleash it onto other people's performances, becoming the villain they loathe.

Words of Advice ★★★★★★★★★★★★★★★★★★★★★★★★★★★★

Instead of getting caught up in all the drama, stay at home once a week and enjoy some alone time. Relish a bubble bath, read a good book, or do a crossword puzzle—find a space that's just your own. You'll be energized by the experience and ready to face your public afterward.

CHOSEN ADVENTURER

Glossary Code: CA

In this ordinary existence, Chosen Adventurers suffer from boredom, and their talents are undetected by others. Suddenly, they are dragged into an epic adventure, chosen by fate to lead an army against an indestructible villain. They're up to the challenge, but when faced with a tough decision, Adventurers can become momentarily paralyzed. Once they take a leap of faith, they find success.

Chosen Adventurers are driven to learn more about the world, fueled by a strong sense of curiosity. They tend to be open-minded and like to feel the blood pumping through their veins. Adventurers are daring, cultured, and bold. As Bilbo Baggins says in *The Lord of the Rings*, "You step onto the road, and if you don't keep your feet, there's no knowing where you might be swept off to."

Famous Chosen Adventurers

★ Luke Skywalker in *Star Wars*
★ Indiana Jones in *Raiders of the Lost Ark*
★ Joan Wilder in *Romancing the Stone*
★ Frodo Baggins in *The Lord of the Rings*
★ Judah Ben-Hur in *Ben-Hur*
★ Yu Shu Lien in *Crouching Tiger, Hidden Dragon*

Chosen Adventurer Typecasting

★ Harrison Ford
★ Kathleen Turner
★ Charlton Heston
★ Jet Li
★ Russell Crowe
★ Naomi Watts

Personality Strengths ★★★★★★★★★★★★★★★★★★★★★★★★★★★

No matter the situation, Adventurers get the job done. Times may be hard, but their character and integrity always stay the same. Adventurers are at their best when they can channel their strength to overcome an obstacle. They might jump face-first out of a plane to overcome their fear of heights, and they'll do it all with a deadpan sense of humor that can make even the most jaded witness crack a smile.

Adventurers are open to new experiences, and they're extremely confident when meeting new people. They respect the diversity of the world and treat the earth with a sense of reverence. This is why they readily find wise souls to mentor them in their careers and life.

If someone needs rescuing, an Adventurer is the one to do the job. When an old lady is waiting to cross the street, it's an Adventurer who will make sure she gets across safely. When Adventurers witness a car crash, they don't think twice about rushing in to help. They possess the rare quality of performing noble acts purely by reflex. In this way, they really are out to save the world.

QUINTESSENTIAL STATEMENTS

"Roads? Where we're going we don't need . . . roads."—Dr. Emmett "Doc" Brown in *Back to the Future II*

"If you were waiting for the opportune moment, that was it."—Jack Sparrow in *Pirates of the Caribbean: The Curse of the Black Pearl*

"The United States Government just asked us to save the world. Anyone wanna say no?"—Harry Stamper in *Armageddon*

"Three weeks from now, I will be harvesting my crops. Imagine where you will be, and it will be so."—Maximus in *Gladiator*

"No matter how many times you save the world, it always manages to get back in jeopardy again."—Mr. Incredible in *The Incredibles*

Personality Weaknesses ★★★★★★★★★★★★★★★★★★★★★★★★

Though they easily succeed in physical challenges, Adventurers find themselves vulnerable in emotional situations. They're used to getting their way by being headstrong—that old lady's getting help crossing the street whether she likes it or not! This attitude works for them most of the time, but it isn't always appropriate in delicate emotional situations. When someone close to them craves empathy, an Adventurer can become very matter-of-fact. Their demeanor comes across as gruff even though they don't mean to be; If you didn't want their advice, why did you complain to them in the first place?

Their natural restlessness is a major aspect of their daring personality, but it can make their lives difficult. They are so quick to take on new skills that other people seem painfully slow in comparison. "What's taking so long?!" is a thought that often rushes through their minds. If the television is on the fritz, they're tempted to throw it away before tinkering with it. This impatience translates into a quick temper that can also be directed at those around them. That's not to say that they'd throw a person in the garbage—but it depends on the person.

TYPICAL MODES OF TRANSPORTATION

Chariot ★ Interplanetary spacecraft ★ Sea monster ★ Back of a dinosaur ★ A plane filled with snakes

CULINARY FAVORITES

Monkey brains ★ Twigs and berries ★ Swamp food ★ Alien stew ★ Fried octopus ★ Roast beast

Their Deepest Secret ★★★★★★★★★★★★★★★★★★★★★★★★

While Adventurers pride themselves on being strong-willed and self-reliant, they actually worry a lot. They may appear to have it all together, but on the inside, they're unraveling from stress. Adventurers really do want to vent their frustrations, doubts, and concerns to a trusted partner, but they seldom do. This is because they are proud individuals who don't like to think of themselves as weak in any way. In the end, they can't find relief from their worries because they won't allow themselves the chance. Over time, they will feel misunderstood as a result.

Chosen Adventurers at Work ★ ★ ★ ★ ★ ★ ★ ★ ★ ★ ★ ★ ★ ★ ★ ★ ★ ★ ★

Adventurers tend to prefer careers where they can share their accumulated knowledge with others, whether as teachers, diplomats, lawyers, or doctors. They love to push themselves in their careers, and they tend to achieve a lot in a short amount of time. They have loads of discipline, and they're great at planning ahead.

Adventurers are generally admired by coworkers as being honest, diplomatic, and quick-witted. If there's a visiting businessman who needs to be taken to lunch, everyone will ask the Adventurer to do it. The Adventurer will nimbly handle chopsticks, eat haggis, or do whatever it takes to close the deal. Coworkers both admire and envy Adventurers for their natural confidence and adaptability.

Adventurers project a self-assured quality that catches the eye of their superiors. Bosses tend to admire their firm character. However, if an Adventurer is unhappy with a boss's decision, they will make it known. They tend to resent not getting their way.

QUINTESSENTIAL BEHAVIOR

Walking barefoot across the desert. ✶ Hopping in a time machine. ✶ Traveling through uncharted territories ✶ Befriending freakish yet friendly creatures. ✶ Staying on a mountain for forty days and forty nights. ✶ Decapitating a foe with a shiny blade. ✶ Liberating a nation from bondage. ✶ Chasing a villain across a rooftop.

Chosen Adventurers with Friends ★ ★ ★ ★ ★ ★ ★ ★ ★ ★ ★ ★ ★ ★ ★

Friends see Adventurers as friendly, soulful, and intelligent. They can act as motivators; an Adventurer may force you to spend the night in the freezing desert to enjoy the stars, and despite your initial resistance, you'll thank them for it later.

Friends can always count on Adventurers to be trustworthy; they never reveal more than they should about their friends, and they always say the right thing to everyone. They are highly sensitive to the unspoken rules of friendship (for instance, they're not going to spill the beans when they know a friend is having an affair). You certainly won't need to kick them under the dinner table; more likely, they'll be kicking you.

Friends can't always count on Adventurers to remain upbeat. During a road trip, they may give someone the silent treatment across five states because they're not driving fast enough. If the waiter is taking too long to bring the food, an Adventurer may be tempted to leave the restaurant. This can lead to petty conflicts that end up making the time go even slower.

MUST-SEE MOVIES FOR
CHOSEN ADVENTURERS

Chosen Adventurers like their movies to center around heroic quests that inevitably end in the rescue of a loved one, a cherished object, or the entire world. They tend to prefer heroes who look tough on the outside but who also have a soft spot for those (animals, aliens, and robots) who gain their respect.

Batman Begins (2005)
Castle of Cagliostro (1979)
Clash of the Titans (1981)
Hero (2002)
Hudson Hawk (1991)

King Kong (2005)
Labyrinth (1986)
The Last Starfighter (1984)
Lawrence of Arabia (1962)

The Long Kiss Goodnight (1996)
North by Northwest (1959)
Princess Mononoke (1997)

Chosen Adventurers in Love ★★★★★★★★★★★★★★★★★★★

People are attracted to Adventurers because they are active, friendly, and brave. Adventurers will consider dating anyone, no matter what race, creed, or culture. They only demand that their lovers have the energy to keep up with them out in the world—and in the bedroom. As a result, they're never at a loss for new suitors seeking excitement.

Adventurers have a more difficult time in long-term relationships. Because they are so confident, they believe they can make any relationship work, even with the entirely wrong type of person. They fare well with partners who aren't afraid to express their love physically, but they should avoid lovers who are emotionally high-strung.

Once Adventurers find true love in a trusted companion, they want to include their mate in all their adventures. When this finally happens, look out, lover!

Most Compatible Cinescope Types ★★★★★★★★★★★★★★★

The Loyal Warrior. Loyal Warriors are built to go on adventures. They're tough, they're willing, and they're genuinely likable. Whether Adventurers desire this loyalty is beside the point—they're going to get it! Both personality types are stubborn and determined to make it work. Together, they can accomplish great things. In *Star Wars*, Luke Skywalker (Adventurer) found this stability in his twin, Leia (Warrior).

Youthful Sages make great smart-ass sidekicks to Adventurers. These heroes bond through their sharpened wit in tough situations. Sages and Adventurers both have endless wisdom to share, and both possess practical skills that get them out of jams. Together, they could have a lot of fun roaming the earth, just like Batman (Adventurer) and Robin (Sage).

Least Compatible Cinescope Type ★★★★★★★★★★★★★★★★

The Enlightened Healer. Healers see Adventurers as lonely, wounded birds, and Adventurers see Healers as overbearing fuss-pots. Both want to play the role of rescuer, and neither likes being rescued. The only way this combination could ever work is in a scenario akin to the situation in *The English Patient*, where Count Laszlo de Almasy (Adventurer) has one foot in the grave before he'll even talk to nurse Hana (Healer). Frankly, it wouldn't make for a very thrilling affair.

Other Cinescope Types Who Have the Travel Bug ★★★★★★★★

Destined Hunters and **Charismatic Performers** share the Adventurer's yearning to visit far-off lands. Hunters don't mind roughing it in hostels, Performers tend to prefer five-star hotels, and Adventurers could go either way—they like seeing all aspects of a new city. Hunters and Adventurers both crave physical challenges, which can lead to intensity in the bedroom. Performers and Adventurers share a love for the exotic, but other aspects of their personalities lead to conflicts in love. Nevertheless, these two types would have interesting conversations during a layover in an airport bar.

Other Cinescope Types Who Are Truly Open-Minded ★★★★★

Respected Champions and **Existential Saviors** are similar to Adventurers in their open-minded approach to people of all kinds. All three types have no problem keeping a conversation going, and they'd enjoy talking to one another. Champions and Adventurers share the tendency to be aggressive, charming, and sarcastic. Together, they'd have a lot of laughs, but neither would take their relationship seriously. Saviors and Adventurers might stimulate each other intellectually, but in romantic relationships both would tend to stray once the initial excitement cooled.

The Chosen Adventurer's Greatest Nemesis ★★★★★★★★★

 The Sneaky Two-Face. Whether in the form of a seductive lover, a tricky friend, or a corrupt thief, Sneaky Two-Faces use their advanced skills of manipulation to lure Adventurers into trusting them, only to reveal their true colors later. Greed is a Two-Face's greatest weakness; Adventurers can use this to their advantage by dangling an object of desire just out of reach, and pulling it away at a critical moment. In *Indiana Jones and the Last Crusade*, the sexy Elsa (Two-Face) wins the heart of Indiana Jones (Adventurer), but she tricks him later.

Why do Adventurers hate Two-Faces so much? Adventurers have a side that is also duplicitous: One foot's in the door and one foot's out. If they maintain this for too long, they could grow a second face.

Words of Advice ★★★★★★★★★★★★★★★★★★★★★★★★★★

Let someone else take control of a social situation once in a while—don't plan anything, make any recommendations, or offer any opinions at all. Let your companion see what it's like to be completely in charge of the adventure for a change! Just take a deep breath, relax, and enjoy the ride.

COURAGEOUS DETECTIVE

Glossary Code: CD

Life's little mysteries can be a real pain in the ass, and the Courageous Detectives of our favorite films lie awake at night tormented by them. These brave heroes scour dark places for answers, engaging in cat-and-mouse games with their adversaries, uncovering the truth under the surface. Whether the villain is a greedy seductress, a master thief, or a vicious murderer, the Courageous Detective always prevails in the end, though the path to the solution always forces the hero to let go of his or her assumptions and face truth's harsh reality. These insightful sleuths know that it's knowledge that can truly set people free. As Courageous Detective Sam Spade said in *The Maltese Falcon*, "We didn't believe your story, Mrs. O'Shaughnessy. We believed your two hundred dollars."

Famous Courageous Detectives

- ★ Sam Spade in *The Maltese Falcon*
- ★ Clarice Starling in *The Silence of the Lambs*
- ★ Doug Carlin in *Déjà Vu*
- ★ Marge Gunderson in *Fargo*
- ★ Catherine Deane in *The Cell*

Courageous Detective Typecasting

- ★ Jack Nicholson
- ★ Jodie Foster
- ★ Humphrey Bogart
- ★ Frances McDormand
- ★ Edward G. Robinson
- ★ Richard Roundtree

Personality Strengths ★★★★★★★★★★★★★★★★★★★★★★★★★

Courageous Detectives are highly perceptive, detail-oriented individuals. A Detective steers clear of dangerous alleys, picks up an item someone's dropped, and comes up with the answer to the riddle that has everyone else stumped. They notice when you change your hair, rearrange the furniture, or alter your coffee-drinking habits.

Using their analytical skills, Detectives read people's intentions well. They possess an uncanny intuition, allowing them to see right into the souls of others. As a general rule, you can't hide anything from Detectives. Always be honest with them, because before long, they'll have sniffed out the truth anyway.

Detectives have the mental prowess to solve the difficult puzzles that frustrate others. They easily figure out crosswords and brainteasers like Sudoku, and they can accurately predict the plot twists and endings of books and movies long before others.

Detectives have a wry sense of humor that can be extremely sexy. They use their sharp wit sparingly, often finding the perfect moment to toss out a scorching one-liner. At parties, they may sit quietly for hours, but when they finally speak they instantly attract attention. Detectives can use this technique to their benefit in romance as well as business. In general, Detectives know how to play their cards to their best advantage.

QUINTESSENTIAL STATEMENTS

"I'm about as popular as a dose of strychnine."—Gilbert in *The Lady Vanishes*

"They think not getting caught in a lie is the same thing as telling the truth?"—Joe Turner in *Three Days of the Condor*

"We're trying to find out who killed him, and where, and with what!"—Wadsworth in *Clue*

"You know, you're the second guy I've met today that seems to think a gat in the hand means the world by the tail."—Philip Marlowe in *The Big Sleep*

"I got the motive, which is money, and the body, which is dead."—Chief Gillespie in *In the Heat of the Night*

Personality Weaknesses ★★★★★★★★★★★★★★★★★★★★★★★★

Constantly analyzing the world around them can leave Detectives feeling worn out. Their determination to finish what they start in the fastest way possible compels them to charge through their days when they need to stop and relax. They're the ones staying late into the night at the office and pulling all-nighters before exams. Fatigue is their greatest enemy, and it can cause them to drop their guard when they are most in need of their critical abilities.

In moments of weariness, Courageous Detectives may become completely incapable of making up their minds. The whole world may seem so overwhelming that even a simple decision like choosing what to eat for dinner will make them irritable and cranky. These moments of intense confusion can be a source of annoyance for people close to the Detectives.

Detectives tend to grow impatient when they perceive stupidity in others, such as in lengthy checkout lines or when waiting for their number to be called at the DMV. They like to be in control of situations rather than left to the devices of less capable individuals. When they feel powerless, they prefer to withdraw into isolation rather than deal with the incompetence of strangers. They might walk into the mall to buy a pair of pants and decide to go home before they even enter a store. Who needs pants, anyway?

TYPICAL MODES OF TRANSPORTATION

Sunbeam Alpine Roadster ★ Orient Express ★ Slinking in the shadows ★ Beat-up jalopy ★ Back of a taxi ★ Carried by thugs

CULINARY FAVORITES

Scotch ★ Gin and juice ★ Cigarettes ★ Cold coffee ★ Donuts ★ Hangover remedy made by butler

Their Deepest Secret ★★★★★★★★★★★★★★★★★★★★★★★★

Deep down, the no-nonsense Detective just wants to let loose and have fun. Whether it's getting a little silly after too many drinks or embarking on a spontaneous night on the town, Detectives crave the opportunity to throw their hands up and announce to the world, "To hell with it!" Beneath their serious remarks and stoic expressions, Courageous Detectives yearn for someone who can draw them out and get them to crack a smile.

Courageous Detectives at Work ★★★★★★★★★★★★★★★★

In the workplace, Detectives tend to make friends with everyone, hoping to find out as much about them as possible. The eyes of the Detective are prone to wander, whether to the computer screen someone is trying to obscure or to the trace of lipstick on someone's collar. Detectives know what's really going on behind closed doors; they keep the knowledge handy in case it's useful, but they seldom gossip. Idle chatter irritates them.

Coworkers tend to think of Detectives as witty, clever, and hardworking. In general, officemates feel comfortable revealing secrets to Detectives. People tend to spill their guts to them, but Detectives like to remain mysterious and discreet about their personal lives, seldom offering juicy gossip in return. Coworkers respect a Detective's natural sense of integrity.

Bosses adore Detectives because they are dependable, detail-oriented, and honorable employees. However, the Detective won't hold back from exposing a boss who behaves badly if justice must be served.

QUINTESSENTIAL BEHAVIOR

Spying on neighbors. ★ Insisting that a relative is a serial killer. ★ Going along with the creepy lady only to turn the tables on her. ★ Working on another hangover before the first one fades. ★ Insulting a lover right before a passionate kiss. ★ Hanging up the phone before someone answers. ★ Revealing the murderer in front of a large, gasping crowd. ★ Making love to someone just to shut them up.

Courageous Detectives with Friends ★★★★★★★★★★★★★★

Though Detectives know a lot of people, they consider most of them acquaintances rather than friends. Once the barrier is broken, however, a Detective considers someone a friend for life.

Detectives are quiet types who often get attention without trying or even wanting it. With their closest friends, they will show a gentler side, a sarcastic wit, and occasional uncontrolled silliness. With acquaintances, they don't reveal much. They prefer to let other people do the revealing first.

Friends of Detectives find them to be genuinely honest and reliable. Detectives give their sincere opinion when asked and are always brave in hazardous situations. However, friends can't count on them to attend cocktail parties, social gatherings, or award ceremonies unless they bargain with them first. It often takes an open bar to seal the deal.

Detectives are creatures of habit, and some might call them a tad predictable. Friends know what Detectives will order for dinner, what drink they'll be having, and what time they will head home. Still, friends can seldom predict what Detectives will say at any given moment. They both love and hate this about Detectives—friends never know when a Detective might say something truthful that no one really wants to hear.

MUST-SEE MOVIES FOR
COURAGEOUS DETECTIVES

Courageous Detectives like movies to have a deep message and a big reveal at the end. They delight in watching a mystery unravel, and it gives them a sense of closure to see a hero systematically expose others for what they truly are.

Blow Out (1981)	*Murder by Death* (1976)	*Sorry, Wrong Number*
Blue Velvet (1986)	*Rashomon* (1950)	(1948)
Brick (2005)	*Shaft* (1971)	*The Third Man* (1949)
JFK (1991)	*Sleuth* (1972)	*The Wicker Man* (1973)
The Lady Vanishes (1938)		

Courageous Detectives in Love ★★★★★★★★★★★★★★★★★

In matters of love, there are contradictions between what Detectives show on the outside and what they're really thinking. To protect their emotions, they may do the opposite of what they are feeling, acting cold and gruff to a person they really like, or turning on the charm for someone they find repulsive.

When momentarily left alone in someone's house on a first date, a Courageous Detective will peek into the bathroom cabinet to see what prescription medications lurk inside. They'll notice when a diary is lying on the floor and when dirty laundry is shoved under the bed. They like things to be orderly, and a messy house makes them uneasy. At the end of the date, the Detective will make the first move, if only to stop the conversation.

Detectives crave an exciting, seductive chase, but they also crave consistency. This dichotomy can spark conflict in long-term relationships. They like to know the whereabouts of their mate at all times, but they will grow bored if the situation becomes too predictable. Revealing a little while remaining mysterious is the key to a Detective's heart.

Most Compatible Cinescope Types ★★★★★★★★★★★★★★★★

The Magical Creator. Creators are unpredictable and spontaneous. They tend to behave erratically, and their wackiness puzzles the linear, straitlaced Detective. Magical Creators may drink too much and wear a lampshade as a hat, prompting the Detective to lie awake wondering, "Why did that person wear a lampshade as a hat?" Though the impulsive nature of Creators will bother Detectives endlessly, it will also pique their interest. These personality types share a love of mystery and witty banter, so when they romance one another, they use surprise as an aphrodisiac. Their relationship is based on the chase, much like the friendship shared by Paul Varjack (Detective) and Holly Golightly (Creator) in *Breakfast at Tiffany's*.

The Rebellious Lover. Detectives are entranced by Lovers and can't help but fall for their fiery seduction. Lovers bring alive the sensuality of Detectives, while Detectives provide Lovers with protection and security. The whirlwind affairs between these types can be as intense as the passion between Jack Gittes (Detective) and Evelyn Cross Mulray (Lover) in *Chinatown*.

Least Compatible Cinescope Type ★★★★★★★★★★★★★★★★

The Charismatic Performer. Performers are initially alluring to Detectives, but in time, Detectives sense that the Performer's show is a smokescreen to divert attention from his true personality. Performers tend to be social butterflies, whereas Detectives prefer staying home in a darkened room. As a result, these heroes tend to drive each other nuts, much like Madeline (Performer) drove Scottie Ferguson (Detective) completely insane with her theatrics in *Vertigo*.

Other Cinescope Types Who Think Too Much for Their Own Good
★★★★★★★★★★★★★★★★★★★★★★★★★★★★★★★★★★★★★★

Existential Saviors and **Vivacious Romantics** share the Detective's trait of overusing their brains to the point of mental exhaustion. Saviors and Detectives are both on a search for meaning and truth, but they approach their quest in different ways. Saviors have a lackadaisical manner of truth-seeking, while Detectives navigate the muck more rationally. Saviors and Detectives make great friends, but they fail to click in love.

Romantics and Detectives are highly sensitive types who pick up on subtle cues effortlessly. They both tend to let little things eat away at them, and as a result, they often have trouble relaxing. In love, these types only heighten each another's anxiety through their shared tendency to overanalyze their actions and thoughts.

Other Cinescope Types Who Are Unusually Brave in the Face of Danger

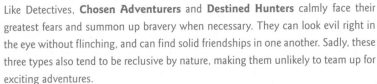

Like Detectives, **Chosen Adventurers** and **Destined Hunters** calmly face their greatest fears and summon up bravery when necessary. They can look evil right in the eye without flinching, and can find solid friendships in one another. Sadly, these three types also tend to be reclusive by nature, making them unlikely to team up for exciting adventures.

The Courageous Detective's Greatest Nemesis

The Nefarious Mastermind. Driven by a thirst for world domination, Nefarious Masterminds lie, cheat, and steal to acquire power. Whether they take the form of nerdy bullies, competitive coworkers, or cheating lovers, they're always painfully clever and egotistical. Their weakness lies in their unstoppable megalomania and long-winded monologues, like the speeches delivered by Hank Quinlan (Mastermind) in *Touch of Evil*.

Why do Detectives hate Masterminds so much? Detectives hate Masterminds because of their blatant disregard for humanity, scruples, and common decency. Detectives often are self-sacrificing in their actions; Masterminds are always selfish. Both of these types see the bigger truth that the masses cannot fathom. Beneath the surface, both Detectives and Masterminds share a feeling of intellectual superiority over the rest of the human race, and if Detectives aren't careful, they can become as cocky as the villains they loathe.

Words of Advice

Try one new thing a week in order to break out of old habits. Your goal should be to incorporate changes that will lead to personal growth. Summon up the nerve to place yourself way outside your comfort zone. You'll find that new experiences will ignite a lust for life.

DEDICATED IDEALIST

Glossary Code: DI

Nobody understands the power of dreams better than Dedicated Idealists. These enterprising and ambitious people have strong work ethics, but they long to leave their jobs far behind. They harbor fantasies of taking down the Man and rising to the top. Dedicated Idealists have secret goals that drive them. Sometimes they're lofty: Go to Hollywood, join a rock band, get rich quick, or see the world. Other times, they're more humble: Start a family, raise a few kids, retire early, have a really good cup of coffee every morning. They deserve success because they've worked damn hard for it, and they sure as hell can defeat the Man. Or as Margaret says in *Clockwatchers*, "You can't fire me. You don't even know my name."

Famous Dedicated Idealists

★ George Bailey in *It's a Wonderful Life*
★ Peter Gibbons in *Office Space*
★ Tess McGill in *Working Girl*
★ Max Schumacher in *Network*
★ Andy Sachs in *The Devil Wears Prada*
★ Chris Gardner in *The Pursuit of Happyness*

Dedicated Idealist Typecasting

★ Jimmy Stewart
★ Jean Arthur
★ Will Ferrell
★ Emma Thompson
★ Jack Lemmon
★ Toni Collette

Personality Strengths ★★★★★★★★★★★★★★★★★★★★★★★★

When Idealists get inspired, they generate a whirlwind of enthusiasm and dedicate themselves wholly. They've got big ideas and big goals, and their talents support their ambition. Whether it's writing a great novel, taking a trip to Antarctica, or inventing a futuristic contraption, Idealists get endlessly excited about their plans.

When they're in high spirits, Idealists are on top of the world. Their energy and spirit are infectious to anyone around them. Friends, family, and coworkers will want to take part in whatever they're cooking up, and in the end, the Idealist has what it takes to make their ideas work.

Idealists are tirelessly dedicated to their families and friends. Having a close-knit group of reliable people is the key to their success, and they honor this as much as possible. They're determined to give others a piece of the pie and a taste of their dreams!

QUINTESSENTIAL STATEMENTS

"Don't you tell me what I can or can't do! Those days are over! And if I want to have an affair, or play sex games, or do M&Ms, you can't stop me!"—Judy in *Nine to Five*

"I'm not even supposed to be here today!"—Dante in *Clerks*

"I really wouldn't care to scratch your surface, Mr. Kralik, because I know exactly what I'd find. Instead of a heart, a handbag. Instead of a soul, a suitcase. And instead of an intellect, a cigarette lighter . . . which doesn't work."—Klara Novak in *The Shop Around the Corner*

"There ain't going to be any interview and there ain't going to be any story. And that certified check of yours is leaving with me in twenty minutes."—Hildy Johnson in *His Girl Friday*

"This isn't just about typos, tapes, staples, and pencils, is it, Lee?" —Edward in *Secretary*

"I'm not going to work at the Gap for chrissake!"—Lelaina in *Reality Bites*

Personality Weaknesses ★★★★★★★★★★★★★★★★★★★★★★★

Idealists don't react well to unexpected changes in their lives. While they may have dreams of doing crazy things, they actually thrive on structure, balance, and routine. They get irritable when something is thrown off kilter, and it is not unusual for them to become fatalistic: They moved my desk down the hall . . . I should quit! It's raining in Florida . . . cancel the entire vacation! They also tend to lash out at loved ones when money's tight or times are hard—but they will always feel awful about it a few seconds later.

Idealists have problems leaving work at work. Whether it's the jerk who stole their stapler or the guy who cut them off on the freeway, small incidents will often ruin their day. Their loved ones feel the effects of this; everyone can sense an Idealist's mood instantly.

TYPICAL MODES OF TRANSPORTATION

Escalators ★ Fast-track to the top ★ Crowded subway ★ Crowded bus ★
Speeding taxi ★ Pizza delivery truck ★ Running with briefcase in hand

CULINARY FAVORITES

Donuts ★ Spaghetti, drained on a tennis racket ★ Black coffee ★
Omelets ★ Cold dinner ★ Happy Hour ★ Pizza Shooters,
Shrimp Poppers, or Extreme Fajitas

Their Deepest Secret ★★★★★★★★★★★★★★★★★★★★★★★

Idealists get so caught up in the dream they're chasing that they often forget to ask themselves if it's still something they actually want. While their dreams are ambitious, Idealists really wouldn't mind settling for a more modest reality. They tend to like the simple things in life: being around loved ones, having a comfortable couch, eating pancakes at a local diner. While owning a private island sounds great on paper, in reality it wouldn't live up to the fantasy they've turned it into. Somewhere inside of them, Idealists know this, and this realization keeps them grounded.

Dedicated Idealists at Work ★★★★★★★★★★★★★★★★★★★★★★

Idealists are extremely popular with coworkers because they never put on airs. They treat their coworkers like equals, and they approach their job with a solid work ethic. They'll often win the "Employee of the Month" award after just one month on the job.

Even though they dread trudging into the office every morning, they also like to make their work area as comfortable as possible. They'll have their favorite mug, favorite screen-saver, and their favorite position in their favorite chair. Their desk will feel like their home away from home, and they'll often voluntarily put in overtime, only to gripe about it later. If Idealists could show up to work every day dressed in a bathrobe and slippers, they would.

Bosses usually relate to Idealists more than Idealists prefer to admit; after all, under-neath the boss's cold demeanor lives another highly ambitious individual. Idealists tend to look at their bosses with some degree of skepticism. The thought, "I could do that better," will cross their minds frequently.

QUINTESSENTIAL BEHAVIOR

Dancing through the streets after getting a promotion. ★ Wallowing in self-pity after closing a deal. ★ Telling the boss off, throwing papers in the air, and exiting dramatically. ★ Hiding an "Employee of the Month" award from coworkers. ★ Running recklessly through crowded city streets to catch a bus.

Dedicated Idealists with Friends ★ ★ ★ ★ ★ ★ ★ ★ ★ ★ ★ ★ ★ ★ ★ ★ ★

Dedicated Idealists tend to attract people like themselves—those with dreams, plans, and impending projects. Together, these friends support and inspire each other. In business, Idealists can often be too trusting of friends. They won't think twice about cutting a friend in on a good deal; sometimes this works out just fine, but sometimes it leads to regret.

Friends tend to think of Idealists as intelligent, ambitious, and funny. When an Idealist is on a roll, friends find their passion addictive. But when an Idealist is in a funk, he'll throw out endless cynical one-liners, and friends can grow tired of the negativity behind the jokes.

Friends can always go to Idealists when they need advice or inspiration. Idealists help to brainstorm ideas with their loved ones—they'll even spontaneously draw flow charts to illustrate their points. However, friends can't always count on Idealists to be encouraging.

Though they're only trying to help, Idealists may say something harsh about someone else's dream.

Dedicated Idealists in Love ★

People fall for Idealists because of their dedication to loved ones, their good sense of humor, and their natural ambition. Who wouldn't respect someone who works so hard for the money? Even when they're unemployed, Idealists bring a sense of security to a relationship. Sure, things may look grim now, but give them two weeks and they'll be back on top! Everyone wants to be this unsinkable.

Dedicated Idealists work hard to woo their lover in the most practical ways. However, as the relationship heats up, Idealists are swept up in desire and lose their pragmatic approach entirely. The romantic confessions come flooding out, and before they know it, they're engaged. Who knew they were so spontaneous?

Idealists enjoy being in long-term relationships, but they become panicky if they feel the relationship is stagnant. When conflicts arise, Idealists must learn how to resist becoming cynical. If they can see the future positively, everything will work out as in a dream.

MUST-SEE MOVIES FOR
DEDICATED IDEALISTS

Dedicated Idealists like their movies to feature dreamers who quit their day jobs and set out to chase their bliss. After taking on coworkers, bosses, and anyone else who stands in their way, they successfully attain their dreams.

Boiler Room (2000)	The Hudsucker Proxy (1994)	Mr. Smith Goes to Washington (1939)
Glengarry Glen Ross (1992)	Johnny Dangerously (1984)	The Secret of My Succe$s (1987)
Haiku Tunnel (2001)	Kids in the Hall: Brain Candy (1996)	Swimming with Sharks (1994)
How to Get Ahead in Advertising (1989)	The Money Pit (1983)	Tin Men (1987)

Most Compatible Cinescope Types ★★★★★★★★★★★★★★★

 The Vivacious Romantic. Romantics are dreamers about love, Idealists are dreamers about work, and when the two get together, dreams will come true. A Romantic can get fully behind an Idealist's ambition, and an Idealist can fuel a Romantic's excitement about love. Together, they share an unbreakable bond, like C. C. Baxter (Idealist) and Fran Kubelik (Romantic) formed in *The Apartment*.

 Invincible Optimists often fall in love with Idealists. They share a wonderful sense of humor, and they balance one another in times of stress. Optimists can also keep Idealists from growing too negative during bad times. Idealists serve Optimists well, teaching them how to stand up for themselves. In *My Cousin Vinny*, Vinny Gambini (Idealist) and Mona Lisa Vito (Optimist) work as a team to clear Vinny's cousin of an unjust murder charge.

Least Compatible Cinescope Type ★★★★★★★★★★★★★★★★

 The Chosen Adventurer. Adventurers and Idealists both long for freedom, but their ideas of freedom are vastly different. Idealists like to earn their keep by working hard and avoiding self-indulgence. Adventurers tend to truly feel alive when they're self-indulging on vacation. In relationships, Idealists tend to resent Adventurers for their worldly ways. Adventurers see Idealists as too pragmatic and cynical. In *Take Her, She's Mine*, Frank (Idealist) finds out that his teenage daughter Mollie (Adventurer) has vastly different ideas about how to spend his money abroad.

Other Cinescope Types Who Love to Stay at Home ★★★★★★

 Like Idealists, **Courageous Detectives** and **Determined Survivors** feel better at home than they do anywhere else in the world. For Detectives, it's a sanctuary; for Survivors, it's where their heart is; and for Idealists, it's their castle. All three heroes could easily be found drinking at the same neighborhood bar on a Friday night, but their relationships with one another would never move beyond friendship. Survivors and Idealists are too different to get along, and Detectives and Idealists spend too much time at work to give love a chance.

Other Cinescope Types Who Chase Dreams ★★★★★★★★★★★

 Rebellious Lovers and **Charismatic Performers** are similar to Idealists in their quest to attain the unattainable. Lovers see lasting relationships as the unattainable, while career goals are out of reach for Performers and Idealists. As friends, these three could easily get along, but as lovers, these matches might be disasters. Lovers and Performers both like the ups and downs of love, but Idealists need a steady companion to come home to—preferably someone who will have their favorite slippers ready.

The Dedicated Idealist's Greatest Nemesis ★ ★ ★ ★ ★ ★ ★ ★ ★ ★ ★ ★

The Stiff Suit. Suits represent the robots of the corporate world. All they care about is money. To them, people are just human capital, and they treat them as such. Suits are easy to crush because they're completely unhappy and they have nothing to live for outside of work. In *Trading Places*, Mortimer and Randolph Duke represent prototypical Suits who think of people as pawns in a twisted game.

Why do Suits irritate Idealists so much? Suits have the power, money, and control that Idealists strive to achieve. If an Idealist were to accept a Suit's offer to get ahead quickly and forfeit their ideals, they'd soon be wearing a stiff suit of their own.

Words of Advice ★

Every so often, just for the hell of it, splurge on one item that's just for you—not something practical or useful, but something that will make all the hard work seem worthwhile. Spending some of that hard-earned cash on bettering your life isn't always a bad idea. After all, you're allowed to enjoy yourself, too!

DESTINED HUNTER

Glossary Code: DH

Destined Hunters have the ability to look evil right in the eye and tell it where to go. They are drawn to things physical and primitive, whether spending time outdoors or screaming at the top of their lungs. When it really counts, Hunters choose fight over flight, unleashing their inner badasses on their enemies. They are natural thrill seekers—daring, dexterous, and possessing nerves of steel. Even if all they're doing is chewing gum, Hunters impose a dominant presence, and their ultimate challenge may be the ability to face down a monster without becoming a monster themselves. In the end, Destined Hunters must recognize that it is their compassion that sets them apart from the killers they face. In *Predator*, Jesse Ventura's character, Blain, sums up the Destined Hunter philosophy when he says, "I ain't got time to bleed."

Famous Destined Hunters

★ Ripley in *Alien*
★ Melanie Daniels in *The Birds*
★ Blade in *Blade*
★ Captain Willard in *Apocalypse Now*
★ Rambo in *First Blood*
★ Blondie in *The Good, the Bad, and the Ugly*

Destined Hunter Typecasting

★ Sigourney Weaver
★ Clint Eastwood
★ Arnold Schwarzenegger
★ Jamie Lee Curtis
★ Bruce Willis
★ Wesley Snipes
★ Milla Jovovich

Personality Strengths ★★★★★★★★★★★★★★★★★★★★★★★

Hunters naturally possess a courage that other people have to work hard to develop. It may not always be visible in their outward appearance, but when Hunters are at their best, they are fully capable of amazing physical feats. A Hunter's bold demeanor makes their companions feel safe; they project an image that clearly states "You don't want to mess with me."

Hunters are agile and resourceful, and they have little trouble facing adversity. They can confront the problems life throws at them with dignity. In conflicts with friends, Hunters know how to pick their battles. They can settle disputes quickly and easily, silencing those who cross them with a stare that sends shivers down the spine.

Hunters are dedicated individuals who stick to their missions and remain serious about all aspects of their endeavors, no matter how insignificant. They can always be counted on to get a job done, and they never complain.

QUINTESSENTIAL STATEMENTS

"If you hang onto the past, you die a little each day."—Danielle in Cape Fear

"Those of you lucky enough to have your lives—take them with you."—The Bride in Kill Bill, Vol. I

"Go ahead. Make my day."—Harry Callahan in Sudden Impact

"Yeah, I got a deal for you. Come out from that rock you're hiding under, and I'll drive this truck up your ass."—John McClane in Die Hard: With a Vengeance

"Villainy wears many masks, none so dangerous as the mask of virtue."—Ichibod Crane in Sleepy Hollow

"Pain can be controlled—you just disconnect it." —Kyle Reese in The Terminator

Personality Weaknesses ★★★★★★★★★★★★★★★★★★★★★★

Hunters take life seriously—sometimes too seriously. They are paranoid by nature, which leads them to assume the worst. If there's a noise under the bed, Hunters will think it's a monster, even if they won't admit it. They will hatch escape plans for every situation, from earthquakes to holiday parties. This kind of thinking leads to guarded behavior in new situations. They'll wait until everyone else is drunk before they take their first sip. They'll scan a room before they enter it—just in case.

Hunters have the potential to lose their temper quickly. Though they can usually channel their rage into a productive task, such as scrubbing mildew off the bathroom wall, when fatigued, they can fly into a rage. They may snap when they feel as if other people are taking advantage of their hard work. If you take a camping trip with a Hunter, be sure to help pitch the tent, or you might find yourself sleeping out in the cold.

TYPICAL MODES OF TRANSPORTATION

Snowmobile ★ Crawling across enemy lines★ Heavily armed spacecraft ★ Japanese motorcycle ★ Running from vampires ★ Skidding down steep hillsides

CULINARY FAVORITES

Cigarettes ★ Air and water ★ Mysterious liquid in a canteen ★ Raw meat ★ Raw eggs ★ Raw dirt

Their Deepest Secret ★★★★★★★★★★★★★★★★★★★★★★★★★

Underneath it all, Hunters are just big softies who don't want to be living an intense life. They may have an aggressive personality on the exterior, but their true self is warmer and more agreeable than others think. They'd prefer to show an ant the door before stepping on it, but they hide their sensitive side to protect their image. Though they may want a hug, they'll never actually ask for one.

Destined Hunters at Work ★★★★★★★★★★★★★★★★★★★★★★

Destined Hunters are strictly business in the workplace. Efficient and determined, they possess a killer instinct for closing deals and tackling complicated problems. They work hard to meet their own high standards—and to meet the high standards they believe others have for them. This drive can lead them to be workaholics. Hunters stand their ground when people try to take advantage of them, but they are able to maintain the delicate balance between aggression and diplomacy. As a result, they do well in positions of power.

Hunters are usually regarded by their coworkers as skilled, powerful, and intense. In post-work social situations, Hunters reveal their deadpan wit with jabs that can cause their colleagues to cheer them on. Hunters can summon a cutting one-liner when necessary, especially toward those who exhibit a sense of entitlement.

Bosses see Hunters as ideal workers and often help them make their way to the top. However, as natural leaders themselves, Hunters tend to see their own bosses as inadequate.

Destined Hunters with Friends ★★★★★★★★★★★★★★★★★★★★★

Hunters show tremendous concern for the well-being of loved ones, especially when there is trouble afoot. If a friend is in a fight, a Hunter always has her back. Need a ride to the airport? A Hunter will get you there in plenty of time.

Though a Hunter's tough-guy demeanor may hide his true feelings, Hunters view their friendships and relationships sentimentally. They cling to old photographs and keepsakes that represent their happiest moments. In rough times, they draw on such memorabilia for inspiration.

When someone hurts one of their friends, Hunters retaliate quickly. When Hunters are around, everyone in the group is safe.

QUINTESSENTIAL BEHAVIOR

Crawling on belly to avoid gunfire. ★ Spitting to make a point. ★ Joining the FBI. ★ Carrying a sword at all times. ★ Taking part in a Mexican stand-off. ★ Ripping the sleeves off a shirt to show off muscles. ★ Using a .44 Magnum. ★ Muttering a memorable one-liner before slaying the beast.

Destined Hunters in Love ★★★★★★★★★★★★★★★★★★★★★★★

Hunters use primal urges to their advantage on the dating scene. They are confident in their sexuality and their prowess, and they use their self-confidence to its best advantage. They may be gruff, but they sure clean up nice. And don't they know it!

People fall in love with Hunters because of their solid core. Hunters of both genders project a dominant vibe in relationships, taking charge and calling the shots. They're usually the ones at the helm of the relationship, steering it on course.

A Hunter is only truly comfortable in love when able to reveal the cuddly teddy bear beneath the gruff façade. Hunters tend to choose mates who will encourage this tender side to come out. Behind closed doors, Hunters can be intimate, deeply romantic, and expressive. In public, Hunters tend to be reserved; if you see a Hunter engaging in a public display of affection, you know it's true love!

MUST-SEE MOVIES FOR
DESTINED HUNTERS

Destined Hunters like movies with heroes who start as victims but use physical strength, determination, and grit to overcome all odds. In other words, they love to watch someone's righteous rage unleashed upon a chaotic world. Bring on the body count!

Big Trouble in Little China (1986)

Brotherhood of the Wolf (2001)

Cape Fear (1962)

Dawn of the Dead (1978)

Don't Look Now (1973)

Freeway (1996)

Ginger Snaps Back: The Beginning (2004)

Halloween (1978)

The Hitcher (1986)

Manhunter (1986)

Night of the Hunter (1955)

The Thing (1982)

Most Compatible Cinescope Types ★★★★★★★★★★★★★★★

The Determined Survivor. Survivors have also succeeded in surviving the worst life could throw at them. They're tough, they don't complain, and they're ready for anything. Hunters and Survivors make an impressive team, and together they take on the world with passion. Hunters can fulfill a Survivor's need to feel protected, and Survivors can help Hunters by encouraging them to reveal their true feelings, much like Sarah Connor (Survivor) does for Kyle Reese (Hunter) in *The Terminator*.

Chosen Adventurers are often good companions for Hunters, because both like to challenge themselves physically and explore the unknown. They can carve out new paths and take turns playing the aggressive role in a relationship. In the *Lord of the Rings* trilogy, Frodo (Adventurer) and Aragon (Hunter) take turns leading their expedition; ultimately, it's the bond between them that saves Middle Earth.

Least Compatible Cinescope Type ★★★★★★★★★★★★★★★★★★

 Invincible Optimist. Having an Optimist join a hunt is a disaster waiting to happen. Optimists would probably walk straight into the gunfire, and Hunters would fail to understand the humor of the situation. Optimists feel the need to constantly cheer up Hunters, whereas Hunters just want to make Optimists stop talking. In the relationship between Corbin Dallas (Hunter) and Ruby Rhod (Optimist) in *The Fifth Element*, Dallas would do anything to get Rhod to stop smiling.

Other Cinescope Types Who Are Too Serious for Their Own Good ★★★★★★★★★★★★★★★★★★★★★★★★★★★★★★★★

 Like Hunters, **Youthful Sages** and **Courageous Detectives** can sometimes be far too serious. All three types face life with a stoic expression and firm stature, but occasionally they just need to drop the serious act and party. When the three are friends, they enjoy letting their defenses down, but when they pair off for romance, the results can be disastrous. Sages don't embrace their sensuality as much as Hunters, so these two fail to find a spark; Detectives and Hunters constantly jockey for control of the relationship and therefore find themselves in perpetual conflict.

Other Cinescope Types Who Like to Take a Walk on the Dark Side
★★★★★★★★★★★★★★★★★★★★★★★★★★★★★★★★★★★★★

 Enlightened Healers and **Existential Saviors** join Hunters in exposing themselves to the world's seedier elements. Hunters experience darkness by facing their worst fears head-on, Healers witness the darkness by peering into other people's souls, and Saviors explore the darkness they find deep inside themselves. Though these personality types often silently respect one another, Hunters are unlikely to find successful love relationships with either Healers or Saviors. Healers desire more attention than Hunters are likely to provide, and though Hunters and Saviors may have intense sexual chemistry, both need too much space to sustain a long-term relationship.

The Destined Hunter's Greatest Nemesis

 The Irrational Beast. Beasts are primitive and unpredictable, seeking only to destroy. Cruelty is the only motivation for their actions. Their lack of reason will eventually lead Beasts to set their own trap, and it's only a matter of time until a Hunter shows up to deliver a fatal blow. In *Jaws*, the man-eating great white shark went on an irrational killing spree that only Chief Martin Brody (Hunter) could stop. **Why do Beasts annoy Hunters so much?** Beasts enter a calm situation and wreak havoc, and Hunters dread chaos. Both Beasts and Hunters get an adrenaline kick from focusing their rage on something or someone, but Hunters must remain vigilant: If they give into their own rage and lose their compassion, they will become irrational, just like the Beasts they hate.

Words of Advice ★★★★★★★★★★★★★★★★★★★★★★★★★★★★

Explore hobbies that require the use of your hands and body, such as sculpture, painting, or home improvement. Channeling your frustration into the physical construction of things will not only make you feel calmer, it will give you a wonderful sense of accomplishment and pride.

DETERMINED SURVIVOR

Glossary Code: DS

Life can be a bitch. No one knows this better than the Determined Survivors, who have weathered harrowing circumstances and experienced the worst of mankind. Survivors tend to have a quiet and calm demeanor on the outside, but deep down they're focused, intense, and serious. They possess awe-inspiring emotional strength and vast wisdom attained from life experience. When the going gets tough, they can be tempted to surrender to cynicism, but if they can maintain faith in mankind and hope for the future, their inner strength will allow them to achieve great things. As Determined Survivor Andy Dufresne says in *The Shawshank Redemption*, "Get busy livin' or get busy dyin'."

Famous Determined Survivors

★ Andy Dufresne in *The Shawshank Redemption*
★ Scarlett O'Hara in *Gone with the Wind*
★ Christina Crawford in *Mommie Dearest*
★ Tom Wingo in *The Prince of Tides*
★ Mildred Pierce Beragon in *Mildred Pierce*
★ Andrew Largeman in *Garden State*

Determined Survivor Typecasting

★ Elizabeth Taylor
★ Tim Robbins
★ Anthony Hopkins
★ Angela Bassett
★ Daniel Day-Lewis
★ Debra Winger

Personality Strengths ★★★★★★★★★★★★★★★★★★★★★★★★★★★★

Determined Survivors possess a steel will that pushes them through any difficult situation. They seldom lose their cool; they power through hardships by remaining calm and dealing with the tasks at hand with a level head. Has the fire alarm sounded? Follow the Survivor to the nearest exit. With their grounded emotional strength, Determined Survivors can easily motivate and guide others through difficult times.

Survivors have experience navigating stormy waters, so they have useful tools for every situation. They're the types of people who can do a multitude of things very well: They're expert cooks, they're good with numbers, they're good with their hands, and they can systematically plan anything. More than anything, they're experts at handling drama. They're emotional jugglers; they can keep all the balls in the air at once.

Survivors won't back down in verbal conflicts. If they feel they've been wronged, they'll confront the perpetrator right there in the middle of the supermarket—who cares if people stare! In general, Surivors go around making the world an easier place for the rest of us.

QUINTESSENTIAL STATEMENTS

"A heart can be broken, but it will keep beating all the same."—Ninny in *Fried Green Tomatoes*

"You are not special enough to overcome a bad marriage."—Aurora in *Terms of Endearment*

"The more things change, the more they stay the same."—Celie in *The Color Purple*

"Can you hear the heartache in her voice? Can you feel it, Joe?"— Andrew Beckett in *Philadelphia*

"We can't have the happiness of yesterday without the pain of today. That's the deal."—Joy in *Shadowlands*

"You gotta laugh, ain't ya sweetheart? Else you'd cry."—Cynthia in *Secrets & Lies*

Personality Weaknesses ★★★★★★★★★★★★★★★★★★★★★★★★

Survivors don't leave their comfort zones very often. They might dream of daring adventures, but they tend to lead safe lives. They like things to be orderly, on time, and predictable. Survivors need time to adjust to new situations; they can panic when facing the unfamiliar.

Survivors tend to get overly involved with the lives of family members and friends, and they often have complicated love/hate relationships with their parents. At times, they can be so entangled with their loved ones that it's hard for them to feel any individual power. Sometimes, this enmeshment with others gets in the way of their romantic relationships— they may become preoccupied with the kids, grandma, or the elderly upstairs neighbor and neglect their lover as a result.

TYPICAL MODES OF TRANSPORTATION
Convertible on the beach ★ Falling down stairs ★ Limping toward the exit ★ Pushing a baby stroller ★ Crowded bus ★ Walking uphill in a blizzard

CULINARY FAVORITES
Southern cookin' ★ Week-old birthday cake ★ Hot cup of tea ★ Prison food ★ Fried green tomatoes ★ Prozac

Their Deepest Secret ★★★★★★★★★★★★★★★★★★★★★★★★

Survivors take pride in their outwardly calm approach to life, but deep down they want to take a break from being so damn strong all the time. They want to crumble. They want to cry. More importantly, they secretly want to be pampered. As much as they can survive on the bare minimum, they long to be drowning in abundance. Whether it's living the high life in a mansion or basking in the sun on a tropical island, living a life of ease appeals to them. After all, why does life have to be so hard all the time?

Determined Survivors at Work ★★★★★★★★★★★★★★★★★★

Survivors approach their jobs with the same resoluteness with which they approach the rest of their lives. They don't break a sweat over deadlines; they simply do a good job. However, Survivors prefer being at home to being at work; they thrive on feeling the warmth of their families and their friends.

Coworkers tend to see Survivors as caring, kind, and helpful. When Survivors go out to get a cup of coffee, they'll get you a cup, too. If you're struggling with the copier, they'll put down what they're working on and rush to your side. They inspire a protective attitude from others even though they're perfectly capable of taking care of themselves. If the Survivor's ability is ever called into question, coworkers immediately rush to their defense. Bosses love Survivors because they're solid employees. They do their job right the first time—they don't need to be asked twice.

QUINTESSENTIAL BEHAVIOR

Rolling up sleeves and getting dirty. ★ Staying up all night with a sick infant. ★ Climbing a mountain barefoot. ★ Chipping a hole in a prison wall with a tiny chisel. ★ Nursing someone else's hangover. ★ Confronting a cheating lover in a parking lot. ★ Plowing an entire farm alone. ★ Escaping a burning building unharmed.

Determined Survivors with Friends ★ ★ ★ ★ ★ ★ ★ ★ ★ ★ ★ ★ ★ ★ ★

Survivors have wide circles of acquaintances. When meeting new people, they tend to be quiet and coy, but they have no trouble socializing with a large variety of people: young, old, rich, poor. As a result, there are always new people who want to be their friends. These soft-spoken heroes are usually a little reserved, but when they relax, they can be lively and full of jokes. They've got great laughs, and when they let their dry sense of humor show, they're truly at their best.

Friends admire Survivors for their inner strength and the warm friendship they provide. They treat their friends with the utmost respect and are encouraging to them in times of struggle. Survivors also have no trouble stepping out of the spotlight to let it shine on someone else.

Survivors are extremely trustworthy, especially when it comes to personal matters. They can be relied upon to keep secrets, holding onto everyone's scandals and confessions forever, no questions asked. However, they cannot be relied upon to avoid drama. Survivors tend to surround themselves with dramatic people, letting them hang around despite their many tantrums.

Determined Survivors in Love ★★★★★★★★★★★★★★★★★★

Survivors usually begin relationships with a sense of caution and proceed accordingly. They'll rarely be the pursuer, because they secretly like to be pursued. They tend to attract attention with their regal presence. Their passive stance toward love actually works well for them, because people try to draw them out to find out what makes them tick.

Survivors are accustomed to being wooed by active, dominant people who won't take no for an answer. The more persistent the suitor, the further he or she will get. As a result, Survivors tend to pick lovers who may not make the best matches for them. They may be charmed by an aggressive wooer at first, but if the wooing continues for too long, a Survivor will want to escape the drama.

Survivors fare the best in relationships when they take more initiative, both emotionally and physically. When they achieve the right balance, they tend to have extremely loving and enduring relationships.

MUST-SEE MOVIES FOR
DETERMINED SURVIVORS

Determined Survivors like to watch movies that stir up powerful (and often depressing) emotions.

Cold Mountain (2003)
Inherit the Wind (1960)
The Lost Weekend (1945)
My Left Foot (1989)
The Panic in Needle Park (1971)
Rabbit-Proof Fence (2002)

Three Colors Trilogy (Blue, Red, White; 1993–94)
The Virgin Suicides (1999)
Who's Afraid of Virginia Woolf? (1966)

The World According to Garp (1982)
Wrestling Ernest Hemingway (1993)
You Can Count on Me (2000)

Most Compatible Cinescope Types ★★★★★★★★★★★★★★★★

 The Destined Hunter. Though Hunters are aggressive and Survivors tend to be passive, both possess a steely strength that is undisputed by all. Hunters can be silent types also, so they don't worry when a Survivor becomes quiet. These two can communicate nonverbally without much effort. In relationships, they tend to be fiercely protective of one another. In *Night of the Hunter*, Rachel Cooper (Hunter) unleashes her rage in order to protect Pearl and John (Survivors).

 Enlightened Healers are good with the wounded, and Survivors often have emotional scars that need healing. Survivors and Healers are both good at empathizing, and they complement one another well. Healers provide the optimistic hope that a Survivor needs to stay grounded, and Survivors provide the steadfast willpower that Healers need to stay focused. Stingo (Healer) provides similar healing of past wounds for Sophie (Survivor) in *Sophie's Choice*.

Least Compatible Cinescope Type ★★★★★★★★★★★★★★★★★★

 The Respected Champion. Champions like to focus on the upbeat and avoid being serious at any cost. Survivors are the exact opposite: rather than avoiding life's difficult moments, they courageously confront them. Champions tend to irritate Survivors because they'd rather joke around than have a serious discussion. In *He Got Game*, Jake Shuttlesworth (Survivor) has problems connecting with his son, Jesus (Champion), because the two have such different values.

Other Cinescope Types Who Like to Fight Oppression ★★★★★

 Along with Survivors, **Dedicated Idealists** and **Passionate Mavericks** enjoy battling oppressors, whether in the shape of evil parents, evil bosses, or evil suits. All three take on the battle alone, which leads to individual growth but can also result in isolation. Idealists and Survivors could work well together in business, but in love, they would only increase each other's cynicism. Survivors would be too inhibited to appeal to Mavericks, and neither would show much sexual interest in the other.

Other Cinescope Types Who Are Comfortable with a Variety of People ★★★★★★★★★★★★★★★★★★★★★★★★★★★★★★★★★

 Like Survivors, **Chosen Adventurers** and **Youthful Sages** can hang out with just about anyone, regardless of age, race, or status. While Adventurers are more likely to bond with people through external activities, Survivors and Sages tend to connect with people strictly on an emotional level. Sages and Survivors can be close friends, but as lovers, neither would make the first move—it's more likely they'd share a crush but never do anything about it.

The Determined Survivor's Greatest Nemesis ★★★★★★★★

 The Insatiable Sadist. Insatiable Sadists can never torture enough people to satisfy their thirst. They tend to view pain as an art form. They enjoy wielding power over their victims and delight in witnessing their tears. Ultimately, once a victim gains even a little power, the Insatiable Sadist will be defeated. Their power was only illusory—they'd merely convinced someone that they had it. In *What Ever Happened to Baby Jane?*, Jane (Sadist) tortures her sister, Blanche (Survivor), and Blanche endures it because she thinks she has to.

Why do Sadists annoy Survivors so much? Sadists hurt other people because they feel insecure and powerless. In the same way, Survivors can feel defeated inside, and if they ever try to hurt other people to feel more powerful, they'll become like the villains they despise.

Words of Advice ★★★★★★★★★★★★★★★★★★★★★★★★★★★★

Pamper yourself more, run yourself ragged less. Turn off the phone, avoid all e-mails, and resist the temptation to get sucked into other people's problems. Put your feet up and enjoy the silence. It really is golden.

ENLIGHTENED HEALER

Glossary Code: EH

Enlightened Healers provide inspiration in an otherwise dismal world. Their ability to care for others and their nonjudgmental attitude makes them perfect companions to a variety of counterparts. They are wise and altruistic heroes who truly believe in the goodness of people no matter what they've seen or heard. But who is this hero, other than a sympathetic ear? No one quite knows. Perhaps their air of mystery comes from a complicated past that they seldom share. They've carried around regret, and now, in the face of a complete stranger, it haunts them. Ultimately, Enlightened Healers must learn how to forgive themselves so that they, in turn, can be healed.

Famous Enlightened Healers

★ Sister Helen Prejean in *Dead Man Walking*
★ Sean Maguire in *Good Will Hunting*
★ Bernadette Soubirous in *The Song of Bernadette*
★ Karl Childers in *Sling Blade*
★ John Coffey in *The Green Mile*
★ Annie Sullivan in *The Miracle Worker*

Enlightened Healer Typecasting

★ Robin Williams
★ Richard Gere
★ Jessica Lange
★ Morgan Freeman
★ Olivia de Havilland
★ Helen Hunt

Personality Strengths ★★★★★★★★★★★★★★★★★★★★★★★★★

Enlightened Healers act selflessly and nobly toward other people; they are some of the most compassionate and loving people around. When there's trouble, Healers are on the scene, no matter what else is going on in their personal lives. They'll stay on the phone long-distance with a cousin who needs a late-night study partner. They'll be the sounding board for the heartbroken and can pinpoint exactly where the relationship went wrong. Healers are great parents, teachers, friends, and counselors all rolled into one. Perhaps they've known great mentors who have helped them get through tough times. Or perhaps they value the power of empathy above all other traits.

Healers strive to be honest at all times. With so much deception in the world, they bring light to any situation with their natural candor. This is most notably true when they are dishing out advice: "Your father clearly didn't show you enough affection." "You have commitment issues." "If you seriously want to lose weight, put down that banana cream pie!"

QUINTESSENTIAL STATEMENTS

"Good night, you princes of Maine, you kings of New England."—Dr. Wilbur Larch in *The Cider House Rules*

"Carpe Diem, seize the day, boys. Make your lives extraordinary."—John Keating in *Dead Poets Society*

"You must make your own life amongst the living and, whether you meet fair winds or foul, find your own way to harbor in the end."—Captain Daniel Gregg in *The Ghost and Mrs. Muir*

"You treat a disease, you win, you lose. You treat a person I'll guarantee you'll win."—Patch Adams in *Patch Adams*

"I want the last face you see in this world to be the face of love, so you look at me when they do this thing. I'll be the face of love for you."—Sister Helen Prejean in *Dead Man Walking*

"The likelihood of one individual being right increases in direct proportion to the intensity with which others are trying to prove him wrong."—Mr. Jordan in *Heaven Can Wait*

They are much less concerned with their own well-being than with the happiness of others, and though their words may be harsh, Healers hit their target with sharp accuracy. People may get mad at them for it, but they'll thank them later—even if it is twenty years later.

Healers understand human behavior. On a deep level, they understand what people are feeling, and they know how to act accordingly. On a superficial level, they're terrific at bombarding people with compliments that take their breath away.

Personality Weaknesses ★★★★★★★★★★★★★★★★★★★★★★★

While Healers spend much of their time helping others, they tend to neglect their own well-being. If something negative is going on in their lives, they tend to ignore it—that death in the family, that hefty speeding ticket, that fight with their spouse. Try asking them about it, and you won't get much of a response. "Forget about me," the Healer will say, "Let's talk about you!"

Healers are usually the ones in control of the conversation. However, if someone they care about takes a direct swing at them emotionally, their defenses go up, and their temper will snap. While they can dish it out, they can seldom take it. Good luck to the person who accidentally pricks a Healer's defenses! Expletives will be shouted, and crazy words will be spoken, such as: "I will end you!" All this, after something as innocent as "You could really use some new curtains in here."

TYPICAL MODES OF TRANSPORTATION

On a cloud ★ Beat-up car ★ Beat-up bicycle ★ Crowded city bus ★
Back of an ambulance ★ Train ★ Walking while thinking pensively

CULINARY FAVORITES

Crumpets ★ Hot cocoa ★ Cafeteria food ★ Canned meat ★
Sack lunch ★ French fried potaters

Their Deepest Secret ★★★★★★★★★★★★★★★★★★★★★★★

Healers may spend most of their time caring for people, but deep down they know that they are the ones in need of the most healing. Secretly, they wish that someone like them would come along and help them out! It's exhausting to be everyone's confidant all the time. Who's there at the end of the day to listen to their problems? Over time, this can lead to a feeling of resentment toward the human race. Healers never share any personal information, because they want people to dig it out of them. But when people try, Healers often erupt and sound the alarm: "Back off!" Unfortunately, this paradox doesn't get them any closer to what they want.

QUINTESSENTIAL BEHAVIOR

Teaching capoeira to inner-city youth. ★ Teaching math to inner-city youth. ★ Teaching creative writing to inner-city youth. ★ Using laughter to heal the sick. ★ Killing an abusive father and returning to a mental institution. ★ Spouting poetry loudly and often. ★ Leaving the convent to teach children how to sing. ★ Inspiring someone to cry and confess their sins.

Enlightened Healers at Work ★★★★★★★★★★★★★★★★★★★★★

Healers are extremely professional and diplomatic when it comes to work. They bustle with a quiet energy and offer compliments to everyone around them. If you're wearing new perfume, they'll smell it. If you're wearing an engagement ring, they're the first to offer congratulations. They're highly perceptive, and they make others feel noticed . . . and boy, does it work. It's very easy to become addicted to a Healer's praise and attention.

Coworkers tend to think of Healers as caring, sweet, and a little too humble. Give a Healer a compliment, and they'll become flustered and embarrassed. In fact, if you want to make a Healer blush, all you have to say is, "Nice job!" When Healers want to ask for a day off, they may become shy and talk themselves out of it.

Bosses think Healers are wonderful and often go to Healers with problems. Need someone to save the holiday party from disaster? Need someone to run a last-minute errand to Staples? Ask the Healer. As a result, Healers tend to feel underappreciated by their bosses—but they forgive them anyway.

Enlightened Healers with Friends ★★★★★★★★★★★★★★★★★★

Healers are extremely popular with friends; their phones never stop ringing. In fact, more than anyone else, Healers are constantly on the phone—after all, people have problems

24/7. They're such giving souls, but they don't know how to put the cell on vibrate or, heaven forbid, shut it off.

Friends see Healers as the kind of wonderful and motivational friends that everyone wants. Healers are so humble about the way they offer help that people don't even realize they're being healed. Sometimes Healers are too giving, and friends who are self-centered will misuse them. Healers may nurse their wounds and inspire them to accomplish greatness, but two weeks later, no one's calling to thank them for it.

Friends can't always count on Healers to divulge personal information. It takes a lot for a Healer to actually confess something that's private and deep. You might have to harshly taunt it out of them and then . . . duck! Along with the confession, a dictionary might come flying at your head.

MUST-SEE MOVIES FOR
ENLIGHTENED HEALERS

Enlightened Healers enjoy movies that feature a victim in need of serious help. Enter the Healer, the hero who will stop at nothing to help get this person well.

Audrey Rose (1977)	*The Elephant Man*	*Passion Fish* (1992)
Awakenings (1990)	(1980)	*Running with Scissors*
Black Narcissus (1941)	*Iris* (2001)	(2006)
Brian's Song (1971)	*Losing Isaiah* (1995)	*Stand and Deliver* (1988)
The Cooler (2003)	*The Man Without a Face*	*Topper* (1937)
	(1993)	

Enlightened Healers in Love ★ ★ ★ ★ ★ ★ ★ ★ ★ ★ ★ ★ ★ ★ ★ ★ ★ ★ ★

Healers are amazing at winning lovers over. When on a date with a Healer, you are the center of attention. Healers tend to attract people who are in desperate need of help. This can lead to relationship problems right from the start. Not only are Healers drawn toward "lost causes," they also have a stubborn desire to change people for the better. Unfortunately, some people will just not be changed and will resent this approach to the relationship. This dynamic can frustrate and confound a Healer.

If Healers can find somebody who isn't in need of serious help, they dramatically improve their chances of having a long-lasting relationship. With somebody who can give as well as take, Healers will find true happiness.

Most Compatible Cinescope Types ★★★★★★★★★★★★★★★★

Determined Survivors are the most obvious match for Healers. These types are very similar; both get over-involved with other people's problems and both like to avoid the spotlight at any cost. As a result, they understand each other without having to work at it. They share a fiery lust that's been lacking in others they've known. Survivors push Healers to confess, and Healers relieve Survivors of their guilt. Just ask Tom Wingo (Survivor) and Susan Lowenstein (Healer) in *The Prince of Tides*.

The Charismatic Performer. Performers want the spotlight on them whenever possible. Healers are perfectly happy to let them be the social butterflies while they hang back and people-watch. They're often the only people who truly understand Performers and love them for their flaws. Healers help Performers figure out what they're hiding, and Performers teach Healers how to revel in praise. In *Ray*, Della Bea (Healer) helps Ray Charles (Performer) get in touch with his inner self while Ray helps ground her.

Least Compatible Cinescope Type ★★★★★★★★★★★★★★★★

The Passionate Maverick. Mavericks are the last people who want to be saved. They want to handle their problems their way. When faced with a Maverick, a Healer becomes frustrated by a lack of response. When faced with a Healer, a Maverick clams up and acts distant. In *Raging Bull*, Vickie Thailer (Healer) tries to care for Jake La Motta (Maverick), but he returns the favor with anger and resentment. Some people just really don't want to be fixed.

Other Cinescope Types Who Give Honest Opinions ★★★★★★★

Youthful Sages and **Courageous Detectives**, like Healers, find truth much more interesting than fiction. Sages share an understanding of humanity just as Healers do, and they enjoy analyzing odd behavior with Healers. Detectives are naturally honest and enjoy comparing notes with Healers. However, Sages and Detectives don't need coddling; they tend to be more independent than Healers. In love, Sages and Healers stand a chance, but Detectives and Healers don't click.

Other Cinescope Types Who Avoid Their Own Problems ★ ★ ★ ★

Along with Healers, **Loyal Warriors** and **Respected Champions** avoid dealing with their own problems. Warriors constantly get involved in their family's problems. Champions like to throw parties to distract themselves. Healers try to fix everyone else. Healers and Champions can be close friends because a Healer knows how to appeal to a Champion's ego. Warriors and Healers can be dedicated friends who would do anything for each other. In love, both Champions and Warriors tend to lust after people who are more uninhibited.

The Enlightened Healer's Greatest Nemesis ★ ★ ★ ★ ★ ★ ★ ★ ★ ★

The Nosy Know-It-All. Know-It-Alls are always lurking around Healers, watching how they use unorthodox techniques to help people, and they don't like it one bit. To retaliate, they desperately try to smear the reputation of Healers. Ultimately, Know-It-Alls lack real compassion, and this will be their undoing. Nurse Ratched is a frightening Know-It-All who terribly mistreats her patients in *One Flew Over the Cuckoo's Nest*.

Why are Healers so affected by Know-It-Alls? Both want to win the "I told you so!" award of the year. If Healers start to get too pushy about giving advice to everyone they know, they're just a small step away from becoming a Nosy Know-It-All.

Words of Advice ★

Get in touch with your inner badass. Being sensitive comes naturally, so now's the time to get in touch with your aggression. Take a martial arts class, learn kickboxing, or buy a punching bag. Don't worry; it's all in the name of catharsis!

EXISTENTIAL SAVIOR

Glossary Code: ES

Existential Saviors have beautiful minds, and they like to use them. They think about the world's most pressing issues ("How do I stop global warming?"), everyday decisions ("The tuna could be full of mercury; should I order the chicken instead?"), and insignificant details ("Can everyone hear that buzzing or is it just me?!").

Normal, day-to-day life is too predictable for Saviors; they'd prefer to jump into an alternate reality to spice things up, or at least to pass this reality in a life-long soul search. These insightful heroes must realize that they have the power to make the world what they want it to be—that they control their own destiny. In so doing, they will find not only themselves, but also, perhaps, the meaning of life. As Existential Savior Craig Schwartz says in *Being John Malkovich*, "I think. I feel. I suffer."

Famous Existential Saviors

★ Truman Burbank in *The Truman Show*
★ The Dude in *The Big Lebowski*
★ Harold Crick in *Stranger Than Fiction*
★ Neo in *The Matrix*
★ Lester Burnham in *American Beauty*
★ Dorothy Gale in *The Wizard of Oz*

Existential Savior Typecasting

★ Edward Norton
★ Laura Dern
★ Kevin Spacey
★ Jim Carrey
★ Winona Ryder
★ Keanu Reeves
★ Lili Taylor

Personality Strengths ★★★★★★★★★★★★★★★★★★★★★★★★★

Saviors are highly intelligent and inquisitive people who can think on many levels at once. In a Savior's mind, the past, present, and future fit seamlessly together. Their heads are constantly spinning with philosophical theories, burning questions, and creative solutions to problems they encounter. They analyze everything from Nietzsche to Scooby Doo. Ever wonder if the Smurfs are actually crypto-Marxists? Ask a Savior!

When Saviors put their mind to something, they do it to the extreme. If they want to learn Portuguese, they'll play language tapes until they're fluent. If Saviors want to relax, they'll get in the bathtub, put on a eye pillow, and listen to a recording of whale mating calls. They also possess an impressive array of interests and talents. One day they'll rock out to "Free Bird" on a guitar; the next day, they'll explain quantum physics to an old lady on a bus; then, for kicks, they'll knit you a toaster cozy.

Saviors have a firm sense of self-awareness that allows them to develop many skills and relate to a wide variety of people. They aren't afraid to examine their biggest flaws in great detail. They'll honestly admit when they screw up and take steps to avoid repeating the mistake. It's this self-awareness that allows them to follow their passions with great intensity and strength.

QUINTESSENTIAL STATEMENTS

"God came down from Heaven and stopped those mother-fu**in' bullets."—Jules Winfield in *Pulp Fiction*

"The more you drive . . . the less intelligent you are."—Miller in *Repo Man*

"I hope that when the world comes to an end, I can breathe a sigh of relief . . . because there will be so much to look forward to."—Donnie in *Donnie Darko*

"I'm being toyed with by a bunch of depraved children!"—Nicholas Van Orton in *The Game*

"Have you ever been struck by lightning? It hurts."—Donnie Smith in *Magnolia*

Personality Weaknesses ★★★★★★★★★★★★★★★★★★★★★★★★

Because Saviors notice and analyze everything around them, the onslaught of input they receive in an ordinary day can cause Saviors to grow anxious. They can't shut off their nervous thinking, so they grow overwhelmed by the tiny details of life. Anxious thoughts play like a broken record for hours on end, especially at night. Saviors are often afflicted with insomnia, and sleepless nights lead to mental fuzziness during the following days.

When Saviors grow confused, they tend to exhibit odd behavior. These unusually bright heroes can suddenly become absentminded. They'll stare off into space for minutes on end. They may wander around a store for hours, trying to find the battery aisle, only to leave with shoelaces. They may flick burning ash into their lap while driving, then crash into a trashcan.

TYPICAL MODES OF TRANSPORTATION

Teleporting through a portal in time ★ Teleporting through a portal in space ★ Teleporting through a portal in someone's mind ★ Dreaming ★ Touring the subconscious ★ Riding a hallucination

CULINARY FAVORITES

Cold macaroni ★ Mushrooms ★ Milk from milk bar ★ Royale with cheese ★ Gruel in a bucket ★ Tylenol

Their Deepest Secret ★★★★★★★★★★★★★★★★★★★★★★★★

Saviors appear free-spirited and uninhibited, but they actually crave very conventional lifestyles: families, decent jobs, a house with a white picket fence, maybe a dog or two. So much of their personality is about being unique, but deep down they just want to fit in. And they don't want to think so much! Sometimes they fantasize about being dull-witted. They just want to kick back on the couch, eat popcorn, and watch tabloid television . . . and not worry about the state of humanity afterward.

Existential Saviors at Work ★★★★★★★★★★★★★★★★★★★★★★

At work, Existential Saviors are focused and driven. They can concentrate on mind-numbing minutiae, or they can broadly multitask, as long as they are adequately engaged in whatever they're doing. If their minds are not stimulated, a Savior might check out completely. Sure, they'll alphabetize files perfectly, but with about as much gusto as a zombie.

Coworkers think of Saviors as intelligent, charismatic, and sometimes a little bit weird. This is because of a Savior's ability to withdraw into thought so abruptly, a characteristic that can be mistaken for rudeness or conceit. Saviors don't give coworkers too much attention or thought, because work colleagues generally aren't a part of their inner circle.

Bosses appreciate Saviors because they're low-maintenance employees. Give Saviors a task, and you won't have to interact with them until it's completely done. However, when Saviors sour on a job, bosses will find that they're suddenly nowhere to be found. Everyone in the office will claim to have just seen the Savior, and yet no one will know where she is. Maybe she's slipped into a time portal beneath her desk?

QUINTESSENTIAL BEHAVIOR

Waking up from a long, surreal dream. • Having an inexplicable near-death experience. ★ Dreaming of going to Fiji. ★ Suffering from an eternal headache. ★ Inexplicably winding up in Poland. ★ Starting an underground fight club. ★ Talking to an imaginary friend. ★ Saving the world in a very subtle, quiet, and completely unrecognized manner.

Existential Saviors with Friends ★ ★ ★ ★ ★ ★ ★ ★ ★ ★ ★ ★ ★ ★ ★ ★

Existential Saviors tend to have a small, tight-knit group of friends that they rely on. Usually, they surround themselves with people like themselves: dreamers, philosophers, and artists. If you're not in their inner circle, forget about it. And how do you get into the inner circle? Appeal to a Savior's surreal sense of humor—or bond with them on a long mystical quest that may or may not include psychedelic drugs.

Friends tend to think of Saviors as deep, interesting, and talented. They enjoy having Saviors around at parties because they're open-minded individuals who can hang out with anyone; they'll talk to homeless people with as much sincerity as they'd talk to the Queen of England.

Friends delight in a Savior's ability to pontificate on a plethora of subjects, but they will sometimes feel put off by a Savior's tendency to become too self-involved. When a Savior is in a bad mood, the dark clouds gather around him, and it's hard to get him to focus on anything else. Friends can't always count on Saviors to be interested in what others have to say. If they're bored, they won't be able to hide it.

MUST-SEE MOVIES FOR
EXISTENTIAL SAVIORS

Existential Saviors enjoy films that creatively portray abstract concepts. These movies reveal truths about the nature of reality and the human condition, but the best of them also ask more questions than they answer.

Adaptation (2002)	Fear and Loathing in Las	Pi (1998)
Barton Fink (1991)	Vegas (1998)	Sweet Charity (1957)
A Clockwork Orange	Memento (2000)	12 Monkeys (1995)
(1971)	Mothman Prophecies	Vanilla Sky (2001)
Cube (1997)	(2002)	Waking Life (2001)

Existential Saviors in Love ★

When it comes to love, Saviors attract suitors with their burning intensity and alluring minds. People fall for them because they've never met anyone like them before, and they appear to have the potential to change people's lives for the better. Saviors express their love differently from most people, and this can be a real turn-on; they're mysterious, intense, strange, and erotic.

In relationships, Saviors do best with like-minded individuals who constantly stimulate their brains. If they date someone who is intellectually uninspiring, Saviors will become restless and will stray. However, when Saviors meet their mental match, they're strongly committed to making the relationship work. Their drive to understand the world is applied to understanding the intricacies of their relationships.

Saviors are the type who are first to think "I love you" but the last to say it out loud. A Savior might forget his mate's birthday but then present a gift for no occasion whatsoever. One thing is certain: When Saviors are in love, whether the relationship is good or bad, they're losing sleep over it.

Most Compatible Cinescope Types ★★★★★★★★★★★★★★★★

The Loyal Warrior. Warriors follow their loved ones into battle, no matter how strange and twisted the battle. They don't ask questions. Saviors, on the other hand, ask nothing but questions. The two form a great balance and can remain dedicated and passionately in love. Saviors need Warriors to ground them with physicality and solidarity, and Warriors need Saviors to challenge them intellectually and spiritually. Like Walter (Warrior) and The Dude (Savior) in *The Big Lebowski*, the two share a silent bond of understanding that speaks louder than words.

The Vivacious Romantic. Romantics can make a dynamic match for Saviors. Both types tend to make themselves anxious over tiny details. They over-think things, but they also delight in the process of doing so. In this way, like minds attract, and sparks will fly. In *Eternal Sunshine of the Spotless Mind*, Clementine (Romantic) helps ex-boyfriend Joel Barish (Savior) rediscover their love by sparking his surreal self-exploration.

Least Compatible Cinescope Type ★★★★★★★★★★★★★★★★

The Rebellious Lover. Saviors like to think first; Lovers like to feel first. Lovers will act immediately on a gut impulse, while Saviors will argue with their gut instinct for hours before proceeding. Lovers are not plagued by the kind of anxiety that makes Saviors mull over the world's problems; Saviors are not plagued by the kind of impulsiveness that drives Lovers to make mistakes. When these two fall for each other, it leads to romantic ruin, as for Maxine Lund (Lover) and Craig Schwartz (Savior) in *Being John Malkovich*.

Other Cinescope Types Who Enjoy the Bizarre Side of Life ★★

Like Saviors, **Magical Creators** and **Youthful Sages** like to fall down a rabbit hole every so often. Sages take mystical quests, Creators let their imaginations run amok, and Saviors slip into the subconscious realm. These three can engage easily in wild conversations that jump from subject to subject. In long-term relationships, they can evolve into the kind of friends who finish each other's sentences. These three types prefer to spend their time together in artistic activities such as playing bongos and reciting poetry, which may or may not develop into pursuits that are more romantic in nature.

Other Cinescope Types Who Want to Save the World ★★★★★

Like Saviors, **Enlightened Healers** and **Passionate Mavericks** also lend a helping hand to those in need, but these three personalities offer their services in different ways: Healers save others from emotional destruction, Mavericks protect the meek, and Saviors show others how to look at the world differently. However, because all three prefer to be in control of the saving, conflict can arise among them when a crisis emerges, and they're likely to squabble over the best way to solve the problem.

The Existential Savior's Greatest Nemesis ★★★★★★★★★★★

The Omnipotent Puppetmaster. This "godlike" enemy pulls all the strings in the Existential Savior's life, whether in the form of a writer, master computer, or sinister deity. The Puppetmaster lurks at every turn, waiting to direct every move. These controlling villains thrive on having total power over the lives of others and love to endlessly torment their victims. But though they can direct the actions of others, they will never control their souls—and therein lies their weakness. The plans of the Puppetmaster can be foiled by a "puppet" who cuts his own strings, as when Truman (Savior) discovers that Cristof (Puppetmaster) has been acting as the director of his life in *The Truman Show*.

Why do Saviors hate Puppetmasters so much? Saviors ultimately believe in personal freedom, and Puppetmasters represent confinement in thought and action. Puppetmasters are control freaks who believe that their way is the best way, and they force their beliefs on their unwilling subjects. However, when Saviors become too self-involved, they can wind up behaving as selfishly as the villains they despise.

Words of Advice ★★★★★★★★★★★★★★★★★★★★★★★★★

Thinking and stressing are not synonymous. Connect with nature more and worry less. Whether through hiking, meditating, or taking pictures, try to engage in outdoor activities to ground yourself. Take off your shoes and enjoy the feeling of the earth beneath your feet.

INVINCIBLE OPTIMIST

Glossary Code: IO

Invincible Optimists are on a mission to prove that a positive attitude and a winning sense of humor will save the day. Their unbound enthusiasm and gusto for life allow them to face hazardous situations unrestrained by fear. Optimists are easy to spot— they have grins plastered on their faces, and they're quick to laugh. They sing to themselves in the elevator and wave hello to perfect strangers on the street. Optimists are delightful to be around, and they tend to have an endless supply of friends. For the Invincible Optimist, accepting reality can be the hardest challenge of all, but in the end, these heroes can always take a bad situation and turn it into comic gold. As Invincible Optimist Clark Griswold posits in *National Lampoon's Vacation*, "Why aren't we flying? Because getting there is half the fun. You know that."

Famous Invincible Optimists

★ Derek Zoolander in *Zoolander*
★ Clark Griswold in *National Lampoon's Vacation*
★ Blutarski in *Animal House*
★ Elle Woods in *Legally Blonde*
★ Borat Sagdiyev in *Borat*
★ Prince Akeem in *Coming to America*

Invincible Optimist Typecasting

★ Ben Stiller
★ Eddie Murphy
★ Goldie Hawn
★ Reese Witherspoon
★ Chevy Chase
★ Doris Day
★ Steve Martin

Personality Strengths ★★★★★★★★★★★★★★★★★★★★★★★★★★

Optimists' unflagging cheer empowers them to march through even the most difficult times with a smile. While others around them succumb to despair and depression, Optimists fight difficult emotions with their power of positive thinking. These heroes are blessed by the best of luck—Optimists simply feel lucky, and therefore they are. They believe in mind over matter, and it usually works out just peachy for them.

People are drawn to Optimists due to their carefree attitude and joyous nature. If something bad happens, they're the first to provide words of encouragement. Broken leg? It'll get better. Can't afford your bills? Don't worry, the money will come. Didn't get that promotion? You didn't really want it anyway!

Optimists are also entertaining, full of delightful tales of wild adventures that they somehow survived unscathed—like the time they crashed into a cop car and didn't even get a ticket. Their personal stories leave people in hysterics; for Optimists, any subject is fair game for a laugh.

QUINTESSENTIAL STATEMENTS

"I couldn't believe that she knew my name. Some of my best friends didn't know my name."—Ted Stroehmann in *There's Something About Mary*

"Do I know what product I'm selling? No. Do I know what I'm doing today? No. But I'm here, and I'm gonna give it my best shot."—Hansel in *Zoolander*

"For life is quite absurd, and death's the final word, you must always face the curtain with a bow. Forget about your sin, give the audience a grin, enjoy it—it's your last chance anyhow."—Crucified singer, *Monty Python's Life of Brian*

"It's not about how much you weigh, but just being happy with yourself."—Sherman Klump in *The Nutty Professor*

"Remember, men, we're fighting for this woman's honor, which is probably more than she ever did."
—Groucho Marx in *Duck Soup*

Personality Weaknesses ★★★★★★★★★★★★★★★★★★★★★★★★

Optimists see the world through the strongest pair of rose-colored glasses on the market. Their ever-positive outlook keeps them smiling, but it also puts them in danger of being taken advantage of. They hear what they want to hear rather than understanding the truth behind empty promises and words. Their easy and naïve nature makes them easy targets for dishonest lovers, telemarketers, salesmen, and scam artists. Optimists seem to have a sign plastered on their backs that says, "If you are crazy, come talk to me—I'll believe whatever you tell me!"

When things do go wrong, such as a serious crisis or a bad break-up, Optimists are ill-equipped to deal with the situation. They may linger in denial for long periods to avoid facing an unpleasant truth. In extreme situations, they might even crack, unleashing the frustrations they've been repressing for years on an unsuspecting bystander.

TYPICAL MODES OF TRANSPORTATION

Ice cream truck ★ A large shopping cart ★ Used station wagon ★
Parade float ★ Stolen police car ★ Invisible horses

CULINARY FAVORITES

Gum ★ Pizza ★ Whipped cream pie ★
Hot fudge sundae ★ Bananas ★ Spam

Their Deepest Secret ★★★★★★★★★★★★★★★★★★★★★★★★

Optimists don't really want to be the people-pleasers they've become. Deep down in their guts they crave a whine and a moan. Being a bright, bubbly person—a one-person cheerleading squad—at all times is a strain. Optimists want to be free to get upset, enraged, and cranky. They want to be able to curse out the car window at strangers and complain about their job. Most of all, they desperately want to tell anyone who stands in their way to shove off!

Invincible Optimists at Work ★★★★★★★★★★★★★★★★★★★★

Who wouldn't want an Optimist as a coworker? These cheerful folk bring joy to a setting plagued by deadlines and endless tasks. Optimists are the ones forwarding ridiculous clips from YouTube, buying gag gifts for the office holiday party, and posting offensive cartoons on their cubicle walls. Count on the Optimists to bring food to share—donuts, bagels, birthday cake, candy—you name it. If an Optimist can't liven up an office, no one can.

Whatever their line of work, Optimists succeed on sheer vigor. Whether they love their job or hate it, they will always power through their day with a natural energy that requires caffeine in others. Optimists can make any task fun; they'll spontaneously sing power ballads while photocopying and may even slip in a photocopy of their butt as they collate the pages of an important report.

Bosses adore sunshiny Optimists, but Optimists should make sure their bosses don't adore them too much—they can be easy targets of harassment if they don't maintain clear boundaries.

QUINTESSENTIAL BEHAVIOR

Singing an upbeat song about the Spanish Inquisition. ★ Reluctantly taking a job coaching kids' sports, only to get beaten up by the kids. ★ Making a tiny architectural model and believing it's life-size. ★ Putting banana peels in the tailpipe of a car. ★ Walking into a wall, backing up, and walking into the same wall again. ★ Cross-examining witnesses on the subjects of perms and purses. ★ Going on a date with "hair gel" on an ear.

Invincible Optimists with Friends ★★★★★★★★★★★★★★★★★★

Like moths to a flame, people flock to Optimists for companionship at social events. An Optimist's voicemail is usually overflowing with messages from random acquaintances, and they'll have more than a thousand friends on their MySpace page.

Optimists have a hard time being firm with their friends. Need a babysitter? Ask the Optimist. Need someone to round out a dinner party? The Optimist just volunteered. Even Optimists themselves can't understand why they don't say no more often.

Friends tend to see Optimists as funny, cheerful, and entirely too open about sharing details of their lives. At a party, it is not unusual for an Optimist to announce embarrassing details of the previous night's sexual exploits to complete strangers. They like to tell captivating stories to eager audiences, who appreciate their sense of humor and contagious laughter.

MUST-SEE MOVIES FOR
INVINCIBLE OPTIMISTS

Optimists like a story about a happy-go-lucky person who has one misadventure after another without ever being in any real danger. In these films, the hero manages to come out on top without even trying, despite seemingly impossible obstacles.

Airplane (1980)

Ali G Indahouse (2002)

Duck Soup (1933)

Friday (1995)

The Jerk (1979)

Monty Python's Life of Brian (1979)

Planes, Trains and Automobiles (1987)

Steamboat Bill, Jr. (1928)

Stir Crazy (1980)

Stripes (1981)

This Is Spinal Tap (1984)

Wet Hot American Summer (2001)

Invincible Optimists in Love ★

Optimists fall in love the hardest. Being the open-hearted, eager-to-please people that they are, they embrace love with a bear hug. Those lucky enough to receive their affections either fall madly in love with them . . . or run away screaming. Luckily for Optimists, they tend to find solid companions, albeit after their share of romantic mishaps.

Optimists are encouraging with their mates and generous with their affection. They shower their lover with gifts, home cooking, and back rubs. Public displays of affection are also common with Optimists. Forget handholding—they'll jump right in to wet, sloppy kisses at the local pizza place. They often say "I love you" too soon and regret it later. It's ninth grade all over again!

If Optimists can find a lover who shares their positive attitude and upbeat energy, they will enjoy a beautiful, long-lasting relationship that makes others green with envy. However, if Optimists fall for the wrong type, they can find themselves dumped before they even have the chance to ask, "Why?" Optimists don't always have a good instinct for crazies, and they should enter new relationships slowly so they don't fall head over heels—and face first into trouble.

Most Compatible Cinescope Types ★★★★★★★★★★★★★★★★

 The Dedicated Idealist. Optimists and Idealists are both dreamers by nature. Although Idealists tend to be more cynical and Optimists more peppy, both personality types will suffer emotionally if they don't feel that the future is full of possibilities. If an Idealist can drop the cynicism and embrace an Optimist, they will enjoy a reassuring and fruitful relationship. After all, it took angelic Clarence (Optimist) to show defeated George Bailey (Idealist) just how beautiful life really is in *It's a Wonderful Life*.

 The Vivacious Romantic. Optimists and Romantics share the ability to fall in love with the world. Both are trusting, good-natured, and positive personality types who are prone to act a little nutty in the pursuit of their goals. They can understand one another's motivations and enjoy each other's zaniness. A romance between them can be as happy as the best times in the relationship between Alvy Singer (Romantic) and Annie Hall (Optimist) in *Annie Hall*.

Least Compatible Cinescope Type ★★★★★★★★★★★★★★★★

 The Existential Savior. Saviors and Optimists have radically different worldviews. Optimists like to sugarcoat reality to make it easier to digest; Saviors prefer to mull over the truth forever. A Savior would hate to watch an Optimist get taken advantage of, and an Optimist would hate that a Savior requires coffee to enjoy a gorgeous sunrise. As with Albert Markovsky (Optimist) and Caterine Vauban (Savior) in *I Heart Huckabees*, when these personalities try to have a relationship, it ends awkwardly.

Other Cinescope Types Who Are Wildly Extroverted ★★★★★

 Charismatic Performers and **Respected Champions** are similar to Optimists in their tendency to put themselves on display. The three would make a successful comedy troupe, but as friends they will just steal each other's jokes or dates. The spotlight can't hold all three at once, and the struggle among them would clear the room. If they could manage to stay together, their loud and raucous behavior would call attention to them wherever they went.

Other Cinescope Types Who Love with All Their Heart ★★★★

 Like Optimists, **Loyal Warriors** and **Determined Survivors** have an uncanny ability to throw themselves headfirst into love. Optimists turn a blind eye, Warriors never question, and Survivors are caretakers; the combination of these qualities provides for solid friendships full of support and sympathy for one another in their individual romantic pursuits. However, they seldom find a lasting attraction in each other, as Warriors and Survivors crave more adrenaline in a relationship and Optimists crave more idealism. It's best if these three stick to picking apart one another's love interests.

The Invincible Optimist's Greatest Nemesis ★★★★★★★★★★★

The Incompetent Pessimist. These villains are angry at the world and make it their personal mission to wipe the smiles from everyone's face. Pessimists can't find happiness in their own lives, so they're set on making sure no one else finds happiness either. Pessimists will call the cops if the music's too loud and tell the boss if coworkers take an extra-long lunch break. When given the opportunity, they impose rules and regulations on Optimists, trying to beat the happiness out of them.

Of course, Pessimists can do no real harm. They're incompetent at what they do, and they'll always be miserable. Optimists win by default. Just as Mugatu (Pessimist) in *Zoolander* fails to keep Zoolander (Optimist) down, Incompetent Pessimists are blinded by overconfidence and clearly outmatched by Invincible Optimists.

Why do Pessimists annoy Optimists so much? Pessimists are stubbornly determined to ruin things for everyone around them, which stands in direct opposition to an Optimist's desire to lift the spirits of others. However, inside every Optimist there exists a nagging pessimistic voice that grows louder when events take a turn for the worse. If Optimists aren't careful, they can switch from one extreme to the other and give in to cynicism forever.

Words of Advice ★★★★★★★★★★★★★★★★★★★★★★★★★★

Explore your darker side through literature and movies to maintain emotional balance. Once in awhile, read poetry, dress in black, or watch movies like *Interview with the Vampire*. Occasionally exorcising your demons will free you from the burden of always having to be so chipper, allowing you to process your feelings in a more realistic way.

LOYAL WARRIOR

Glossary Code: LW

Loyal Warriors are noble heroes who derive power from an unyielding dedication to others with a common cause. Loyal Warriors believe that life is meant to be shared, and they inspire a sense of unity wherever they go. Warriors are never as happy as when they have loved ones around them. While functioning amid a unit, Warriors must learn to sacrifice parts of themselves for the good of the mission. They must learn how to believe in the strength of their comrades. Loyal Warriors uphold the idea that true success isn't worth having if you can't share it with your friends. As Coach Normal Dale says in *Hoosiers*, "Five players on the floor functioning as one single unit: team, team, team—no one more important than the other."

Famous Loyal Warriors

★ Coach Norman Dale in *Hoosiers*
★ Col. Nicholson in *The Bridge on the River Kwai*
★ Princess Leia in the *Star Wars* series
★ Sgt. Roger Murtaugh in *Lethal Weapon*
★ Captain John Miller in *Saving Private Ryan*
★ King Arthur in *Camelot*

Loyal Warrior Typecasting

★ The Rock
★ Sean Astin
★ Tom Hanks
★ Keira Knightly
★ Mark Wahlberg
★ Jada Pinkett Smith

Personality Strengths ★★★★★★★★★★★★★★★★★★★★★★★★

Loyal Warriors are strong, loving, and secure individuals who care deeply for their loved ones and aren't afraid to show it. If someone needs something done, Warriors will do it, no questions asked. Warriors have a strong sense of nobility. They'll behave like gentility even in the middle of an apocalypse. They'll treat the enemy with respect and the opposite sex with courtesy. People love this about them.

Warriors make fantastic leaders in any group situation. They like to be at the helm of a social ship, guiding it to wherever it's going. They're at their best when rallying a group of people to an event, whether it's a concert, party, or excursion. With social events, they'll make plans for all of their friends, and they will take charge whenever problems arise. If the bill comes up short at dinner, they'll pick up the slack even if they're strapped for cash. If friends are fighting, the Warrior will instantly straighten the situation out and get everyone to group-hug.

Loyal Warriors are social chameleons and the most likeable folks you'll meet. They prefer to adapt to their environment rather than shape the elements to suit their own needs. Wherever they are, whomever they're with, they're having fun.

QUINTESSENTIAL STATEMENTS

"Win one for the Gipper!"—George Gipp in *Knute Rockne, All-American*

"There is another kind of evil that we must fear the most, and that is the indifference of good men."
—Monsignor in *The Boondock Saints*

"Ohana means family, and family means . . . nobody gets left behind or forgotten."—Lilo in *Lilo and Stitch*

"You're my best friend."—Daisy in *Driving Miss Daisy*

"I wish I could say something classy and inspirational, but that just wouldn't be our style."—Shane Falco in *The Replacements*

"You're a lean, mean, fighting machine!"—Dewey "Ox" Oxberger in *Stripes*

Personality Weaknesses ★★★★★★★★★★★★★★★★★★★★★★★

Warriors need others around, and because of this, they struggle with time alone. When the phone stops ringing and everything's completely silent, Warriors feel like jumping out of their skin. If left alone for too long, a Warrior will grow very irritable and frustrated. Warriors really don't know how to enjoy their own company, because they're simply not used to it.

Warriors have high standards for friends and family when it comes to loyalty and generosity. They feel that everyone should be as caring and faithful as they are. If someone makes a negative comment, Warriors will take it to heart like a poisoned arrow. Feeling betrayed is not an uncommon emotion. Warriors can often misread the motives of others and feel betrayed before they have all the facts. Sometimes, they let their paranoia get the best of them.

TYPICAL MODES OF TRANSPORTATION
Unmarked police car ★ Team bus ★ Apache helicopter ★ Tandem
bicycle ★ On the shoulders of teammates ★ In the arms of fellow soldiers

CULINARY FAVORITES
Burger and fries ★ Celebratory pizza ★ Chinese food ★
Beer ★ MRE rations ★ Soul food

Their Deepest Secret ★★★★★★★★★★★★★★★★★★★★★★★★★

Underneath their undying loyalty to loved ones, Warriors are itching to go out on a solo mission. Sure, it's great having friends around, but wouldn't it be nice just to drive out to the mountains and rent that cabin all alone? They desperately want to prove to themselves that solitude can be enjoyable and that they don't need to rely on anyone. This is why they get along with loners so well; there's a part of them that's jealous. Underneath it all, they long for this sort of freedom, and yet they avoid taking it when the opportunity presents itself.

Loyal Warriors at Work ★★★★★★★★★★★★★★★★★★★★★★★

At work, Warriors are right at home. They're agreeable employees who enjoy being part of a team and will do whatever they have to for the group's benefit. They do well in positions of management; they bring out the best in their employees with positive reinforcement.

Coworkers tend to see Warriors as strong, happy, and lovable. They do whatever the group's doing; they never make a fuss or cause a stir. In fact, they avoid drama at all costs. If you want to piss a Warrior off, have a hissy fit over something insignificant, like where to eat lunch.

Bosses love Warriors and often consider them to be equals. They'll confide in Warriors, offering up scandalous secrets that they really shouldn't share. Warriors see bosses as regular people who have the same problems as everyone else.

QUINTESSENTIAL BEHAVIOR

Giving a motivational speech in a locker room. ★ Running across a battlefield to retrieve a wounded soldier. ★ Pushing a broken-down van to a gas station. ★ Driving a herd of cattle with a fellow cowboy. ★ Convincing an athlete to make a comeback. ★ Taking a group trip on a crowded bus. ★ Forging an unlikely friendship with a rival. ★ Filling in for a hurt teammate and scoring a touchdown.

Loyal Warriors with Friends ★★★★★★★★★★★★★★★★★★★★★

Warriors make friends with all types of people without even trying. Put a Warrior with an Existential Savior, and the Warrior will channel her inner philosopher. Put a Warrior with a Chosen Adventurer, and they'll tandem sky-dive out of a plane. Put a Warrior with a Passionate Maverick, and the Warrior will silently respect the Maverick's need for quiet. Consequently, everyone wants a Warrior around.

Warriors tend to take the route of least resistance when it comes to social situations. They can have fun just sitting on a couch watching a game and drinking a beer. They do, however, have boundary problems. Don't be surprised to find a Warrior dog-sitting for an ex-lover or picking up dry cleaning for a roommate.

Friends can always count on Warriors to make it to a party. They'll bring the keg and even help clean up the puke in the bathroom afterward. But watch out: Pissing a Warrior off in front of friends is a bad idea. Once they unleash their rage, it will take five people to pull them off the offending loudmouth.

Loyal Warriors in Love ★★★★★★★★★★★★★★★★★★★★★★★

The wooing process can often make Warriors nervous. These normally extroverted heroes may start to act shy if they're really attracted to someone. When dating, Warriors can become sentimental and romantic. They secretly like love songs and poetry, but they'd never ever let anyone know.

When Warriors find someone to love, they love with all their might. They give themselves up completely and never look back. In marriage, they start families quickly, often having multiple children and/or pets. They like to feel like their home is a bustling place of energy and inspiration, and it's usually full of visiting guests and lingering family members. Warriors who fare best in love learn how to be more independent. Being in a unit comes naturally to them, but taking the time to develop their own interests outside of their mate can strengthen the relationship.

MUST-SEE MOVIES FOR
LOYAL WARRIORS

While most films are about lone heroes with individual journeys, Warriors like movies about heroes who thrive as part of a team. Whether the stories are about war, sports, adventure, or family, these heroes tackle huge obstacles with help from others.

Boyz n the Hood (1991)
Enemy Mine (1985)
First Knight (1995)
Get on the Bus (1996)
Hamburger Hill (1987)

How the West Was Won (1962)
Little Miss Sunshine (2006)
The Longest Yard (1972)

Midnight Run (1988)
Miracle (2004)
The Outsiders (1983)
Paths of Glory (1957)
Remember the Titans (2000)

Most Compatible Cinescope Types ★★★★★★★★★★★★★★★

 The Chosen Adventurer. Adventurers prefer to travel alone, but they'll make an exception for Loyal Warriors because the two get along so well. Warriors will cheerfully support any bold decisions that Adventurers make. Adventurers will teach Warriors how to be confident in their own abilities and attain their dreams. In *The*

Princess Bride, Westley (Adventurer) and Fezzik (Warrior) form a bond while defeating villains.

Existential Saviors make great matches for Warriors. Saviors need someone to be a grounding force in their lives, and Warriors live to be that stabilizing rock. Warriors can grow spiritually with Saviors, and Saviors can learn how to unleash their love with Warriors. In *The Matrix*, Neo (Savior) and Trinity (Warrior) fall in love and define the very nature of existence.

Least Compatible Cinescope Type ★ ★ ★ ★ ★ ★ ★ ★ ★ ★ ★ ★ ★ ★ ★ ★ ★

The Magical Creator. Magical Creators and Warriors might team up when a dragon needs slaying, but in everyday life they drive each other nuts. While both heroes love to have fun, the ongoing social demands in a Warrior's life make a Creator sulky. Likewise, a Creator's impulsivity makes a Warrior cranky. Like the Wizard (Creator) and the Scarecrow (Warrior) in *The Wizard of Oz*, they expose each other's flaws rather than cherish them.

Other Cinescope Types Who Are Social Chameleons ★ ★ ★ ★ ★

Like Warriors, **Enlightened Healers** and **Vivacious Romantics** can be chameleons in social settings. Healers tend to mirror the mood of the person they're with, Romantics tend to impress others by behaving in radically different ways, and Warriors tend to blend into every situation. Healers and Warriors could make wonderful long-term friends, but they wouldn't know how to behave around each other if dating. Romantics and Warriors could easily have sentimental love affairs and enjoy silly love songs together.

Other Cinescope Types Who Are Team Players ★ ★ ★ ★ ★ ★ ★ ★ ★

Along with Warriors, **Respected Champions** and **Dedicated Idealists** are easygoing in group situations. Each of these heroes welcomes other peoples' visions, and none of them feels threatened by the talents of others. If you've got a great idea, these are the heroes to ask for help. Champions and Warriors often fall in love, because they share a strong loyalty and an urge to help the underdog. Idealists and Warriors wouldn't challenge each other enough to spark love, but they'd definitely be friendly coworkers.

The Loyal Warrior's Greatest Nemesis ★★★★★★★★★★★★★

 The Selfish Backstabber. When unity is a necessity for survival, the one villain who can screw things up is a Backstabber. Backstabbers thrive on sabotaging the goals of those around them for personal gain. Ultimately, Backstabbers will be no match for the strength of a unified group. In *Platoon*, Sgt. Bob Barnes is the Backstabber who puts the lives of his fellow soldiers in jeopardy, including Pvt. Chris Taylor (Warrior).

Why do Warriors hate Backstabbers so much? Backstabbers hurt anyone to get ahead, while Warriors would rather hurt themselves than hurt their loved ones. When Warriors feel down, they may be tempted to abandon the team in a time of crisis. If they did, they could become as selfish as the Backstabbers they loathe.

Advice for Loyal Warriors ★★★★★★★★★★★★★★★★★★★★★

Pursue a hobby that can be done entirely on your own. Whether it's running or learning an instrument, try something that doesn't require a posse to complete. A solo activity will help you clear your head and give you a sense of personal power.

MAGICAL CREATOR

Glossary Code: MC

Magical Creators believe that having fun is the most important thing in life. Once these heroes realize they can turn the world into a magical place, they're never the same again. Larger than life, spontaneous, and prone to selfless acts of kindness, they tend to have great laughs and mysterious smiles. Though these energetic and visionary personalities will sometimes hide their talents, they enjoy pushing the boundaries of what society considers normal. Although their intention is to make life more joyful, they also possess an impish urge to meddle that can land them in heaps of trouble. When a Magical Creator is near, expect the unexpected. As Magical Creator Willy Wonka sings in *Willy Wonka and the Chocolate Factory*, "A little nonsense now and then is relished by the wisest men."

Famous Magical Creators

★ Amelie Poulain in *Amelie*
★ Edward Scissorhands in *Edward Scissorhands*
★ Maude in *Harold and Maude*
★ Viktor Frankenstein in *Young Frankenstein*
★ Holly Golightly in *Breakfast at Tiffany's*

Magical Creator Typecasting

★ Gene Wilder
★ Audrey Hepburn
★ Johnny Depp
★ Ruth Gordon
★ Jimmy Stewart
★ Julie Andrews

Personality Strengths ★★★★★★★★★★★★★★★★★★★★★★★★★

Magical Creators have a natural zest for life. Creators strive to appreciate all the little things that make the world beautiful. They see the world as being full of endless possibilities; wherever they go, magic follows.

Creators can suddenly act very silly for no reason. They dance in front of the mirror when no one's looking, sing loudly in the shower, or announce to everyone that they're taking a spontaneous drive to the ocean—right this second! They delight in telling others about their adventures, and others delight in listening. They're so full of stories that it can seem impossible to believe that they've experienced everything they describe.

But strange things happen to everyone when Magical Creators are near—they seem to be followed by a whirlwind of serendipity, and everyone benefits. Old friends pop up after having been out of contact for years, or a wrong turn leads to the discovery of a cool new hangout. But Creators seem completely oblivious to the magic that's happening all around them—for them, it's just normal.

QUINTESSENTIAL STATEMENTS

"Lord, what fools these mortals be!"—Puck in *A Midsummer Night's Dream*

"I think we've got to measure goodness by what we embrace, what we create, and who we include."—Père Henri in *Chocolat*

"You're wearing that hat? After all the magic I used to make your dress pretty?"—Howl in *Howl's Moving Castle*

"I always have a wonderful time, wherever I am, whoever I'm with."
—Elwood P. Dowd in *Harvey*

"In every job that must be done, there is an element of fun. You find the fun and snap! the job's a game."—Mary Poppins in *Mary Poppins*

"Pay no attention to that man behind the curtain."—The Wizard in *The Wizard of Oz*

Personality Weaknesses ★★★★★★★★★★★★★★★★★★★★★★★

Living in a world of spontaneous adventure can be maddening and chaotic. Magical Creators can't stop running on high octane, and their enthusiasm can be exhausting to friends and loved ones. Driving to Vegas in the middle of the night may seem like a fun idea at first, but its appeal dwindles by the third hour of the journey. The Creator's frantic pace can bring on bouts of moodiness, and when a Creator isn't having fun, no one is.

Although they appear to be social, Creators like to remain isolated and aloof, and their own comfort level dictates how well they'll let others know them. Therefore, it's easier for the Magical Creator to host the party than to attend it. As host, a Creator can ensure that everyone's having a blast, but as an attendee, a Creator may suddenly get pouty or even vanish into thin air, abandoning those who were counting on a ride home.

TYPICAL MODES OF TRANSPORTATION
Time machine ★ Broomstick ★ Glass elevator ★
Dragon ★ Hot air balloon ★ Puff of smoke

CULINARY FAVORITES
Witch's brew ★ Spoonful of sugar ★ Everlasting gobstoppers ★
Magical, aphrodisiac chocolate ★ An endless buffet of
beautiful and delicious food

Their Deepest Secret ★★★★★★★★★★★★★★★★★★★★★★★

Underneath the Creator's fun-loving exterior is an introvert who both craves and fears attention. Creators want to be intimate, but they also want to be alone. They are simultaneously afraid and desirous of meeting someone who will discover their true self. This ambiguity manifests in all sorts of odd behavior. For example, if a Creator feels a real connection developing with another person, she may suddenly announce that she forgot to turn off her stove and walk away mid-conversation.

Magical Creators at Work ★★★★★★★★★★★★★★★★★★★★★

Magical Creators are lively, humorous, and generous coworkers. People like to have them around. They enjoy the fun that Creators provide, and they like to gossip about their antics. Creators are a load of laughs at holiday parties, and they spice up the office gift exchange with the strange gifts everyone remembers, like left-handed combs and hand massagers.

When their job allows them to use their talent and creativity, Creators will rise to the top without much effort. However, boredom is a Creator's worst enemy. If their talents aren't put to use, they will jump from job to job in search of excitement. Jobs that mainly consist of tedious tasks such as filing, data entry, or monotonous factory work are unlikely to fulfill the Creator's constant need for stimulation.

Bosses tend to have mixed feelings toward Creators. They respect their ability to perform miracles under pressure, but they worry that Creators will spontaneously quit if something new and exciting comes along.

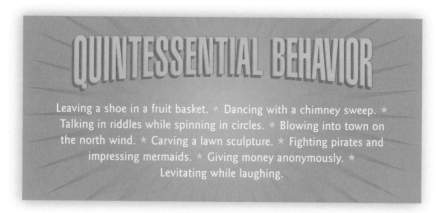

QUINTESSENTIAL BEHAVIOR

Leaving a shoe in a fruit basket. ★ Dancing with a chimney sweep. ★ Talking in riddles while spinning in circles. ★ Blowing into town on the north wind. ★ Carving a lawn sculpture. ★ Fighting pirates and impressing mermaids. ★ Giving money anonymously. ★ Levitating while laughing.

Magical Creators with Friends ★★★★★★★★★★★★★★★★★★★

Friends of Creators know them to be generous, funny, and impulsive. Friends adore Creators' excitement for life. Creators are always up for spur-of-the-moment fun, whether it's an impromptu expedition to the outskirts of nowhere or an exotic dinner. However, Creators can be highly sensitive, and friends sometimes find it hard to anticipate their reactions to seemingly harmless situations. Though a surprise birthday party seems perfect for a Creator, there's a good chance it would end in disaster due to Creators' unpredictability in social settings.

Friends can count on Creators to give them the types of remarkable presents that no one else would even think of. Hearing the delighted squeals in response gives Creators a sense of fulfillment.

Magical Creators in Love ★★★★★★★★★★★★★★★★★★★★★★★★★★

Magic and love go hand in hand, so it's natural for Creators to experience whirlwind romances. They tend to have the kind of fantasy first dates that others only dream about. Snow will fall on cue. Music will emerge from a small café. A kiss will be perfectly timed to the setting sun. Falling in love with a Creator seems like the easiest thing in the world.

Long-term relationships are a different story. A Creator's unpredictability can be a source of conflict in longer affairs. When the relationship stops being a constant source of fun and excitement, Creators can grow volatile. They may suddenly pack their bags and leave in a huff, only to return a few days later as though nothing happened, causing confusion in even the most confident, steadfast partner.

The best-suited lovers for Creators use silliness and good, old-fashioned fun to capture their hearts. Ultimately, Creators are easy to please once a successful mate unlocks the mystery of their impulsive personality.

MUST-SEE MOVIES FOR MAGICAL CREATORS

Magical Creators like movies that provide an escape from everyday life and plunge them into the vastness of imagination, with heroes who alter the world for the better and make sure that everyone has a good time along the way.

The Adventures of Baron Munchausen (1989)

Cinema Paradiso (1988)

The Dark Crystal (1982)

Labyrinth (1986)

Like Water for Chocolate (1992)

Orlando (1992)

Pan's Labyrinth (2007)

Pee-wee's Big Adventure (1985)

The Science of Sleep (2006)

The Witches of Eastwick (1987)

The Wizard of Speed and Time (1989)

You Can't Take It with You (1938)

Most Compatible Cinescope Types ★★★★★★★★★★★★★★★★

 The Courageous Detective. Only sleuths have the patience and tenacious desire to discover what makes Creators tick. Creators are wild and Detectives are steady, so they balance each other out. There's something mysterious about the way both of these personalities woo, and they enjoy surprising one another. Their romance is fueled by the chase, much like the interaction between Amélie (Creator) and Nino (Detective) in *Amélie*.

Youthful Sages also make great companions for Creators, since both heroes can appreciate the mystical side of life. Underneath it all, Creators and Sages are just big kids who hate to follow the rules. Together they can have wild adventures while solving the world's problems, as exemplified by Professor Dumbledore (Creator) and Harry Potter (Sage) in *Harry Potter and the Sorcerer's Stone*.

Least Compatible Cinescope Type ★★★★★★★★★★★★★★★★★★

The Determined Survivor. Survivors have seen the dark side of life—they've experienced bad events and lived to tell about them. They're a reminder of all the things Creators try to avoid. Creators can't stand to see sadness, and they go to great lengths to avoid it. Survivors and Creators tend to clash much like Hans Wilhelm Friederich Kemp (Survivor) and Viktor Frankenstein (Creator) in *Young Frankenstein*.

Other Cinescope Types Who Live for the Moment ★★★★★★★★

Like Creators, **Rebellious Lovers** and **Passionate Mavericks** tend to live life in short bursts instead of in long strides. The three types share an intense love of thrills and wild escapades, and so long as they can appreciate the Creator's unique sense of humor, these three can get along well. Rebellious Lovers are often attracted to outsiders, so Creators fit their ideal. Passionate Mavericks and Magical Creators are uninhibited by the opinions of others, and as a result, they might even fall for one another.

Other Cinescope Types Who Are Mischievous ★★★★★★★★★

Vivacious Romantics and **Respected Champions** are as prone to make mischief as Magical Creators. Romantics are driven to wacky antics in the pursuit of love, while Champions are usually driven to puckish acts to defeat bullies. These person-alities can make each other laugh for hours on end. They tend to be good friends who delight in playing well-conceived practical jokes on one another, but they're better off as friends than lovers.

The Magical Creator's Greatest Nemesis ★★★★★★★★★★★★

 The Uptight Killjoy. It is the mission of Uptight Killjoys to silence creativity wherever it abounds. Whether they take the form of sadistic headmasters, disciplinarians, or strict parents, they are always conformist to a fault. Their weakness lies in their unflinching rigidity; when faced with proof that a world exists outside of their beliefs, Killjoys crumble. In *Peter Pan*, Captain Hook is a Killjoy who winds up defeated by the sprightly Creator Peter Pan.

Why do Killjoys annoy Creators so much? Beneath the wild behavior, Creators desperately want to help other people, and they can't stand that Killjoys lack this empathetic desire. However, both personality types tend to live in extremes, and if Creators aren't careful, they might become as strict about enforcing fun as Killjoys are about enforcing misery.

Advice for Magical Creators ★★★★★★★★★★★★★★★★★★★★

Although it may seem as if you have to cast magical spells for everything to work out, sometimes allowing things to take their natural course brings the most miraculous results. Find a regular time to relax somewhere beautiful and just let things happen around you.

PASSIONATE MAVERICK

Glossary Code: PM

Passionate Mavericks are like fish swimming against the current. The masses may be telling them what to do, who to love, or how to behave, but these rebels choose not to listen. They're dissatisfied with the status quo, and, on behalf of the meek and the voiceless, they want to change the world for the better. Mavericks don't follow trends—they set them. They're cool without even trying. They have hordes of people who fear and admire them, but they're loners by nature and often keep their distance. In the end, Mavericks must realize that accepting help from others only makes their mission stronger. In the words of Passionate Maverick William Wallace in *Braveheart*, "They may take our lives, but they'll never take our freedom!"

Famous Passionate Mavericks

★ Josey Aimes in *North Country*
★ William Wallace in *Braveheart*
★ Tony Montana in *Scarface*
★ Louise Sawyer in *Thelma and Louise*
★ Butch Cassidy in *Butch Cassidy and the Sundance Kid*
★ Henry Hill in *Goodfellas*

Passionate Maverick Typecasting

★ Paul Newman
★ Julia Roberts
★ James Dean
★ Robert DeNiro
★ Charlize Theron
★ Susan Sarandon

Personality Strengths ★★★★★★★★★★★★★★★★★★★★★★★★★★

Mavericks are fiercely driven, inspired, and committed people. Once Mavericks make a decision, they refuse to let anything stand in their way. In extreme cases, Mavericks may even resort to aggression to achieve their objectives.

Mavericks work hard, play hard, and love hard, pressing ahead as though there's fire in their bellies. They're go-getters who take the initiative in any situation—they don't have time to wait for other people to make the first move.

Mavericks are a vocal bunch who don't shy away from making their feelings and ideas heard. In casual conversation, they're fearless in expressing their opinions, especially regarding politics and world issues. They don't care who they offend or anger, and in general, they act like they don't care what others think—an attitude that is the very definition of cool.

QUINTESSENTIAL STATEMENTS

"At this point, we ain't headed to nowhere. We're just runnin' from." —Clyde Barrow in *Bonnie and Clyde*

"It's not personal, Sonny. It's strictly business."—Michael Corleone in *The Godfather*

"If I had one day when I didn't have to be all confused, and I didn't have to feel that I was ashamed of everything . . . if I felt that I belonged someplace . . . you know?"—Jim

Stark in *Rebel Without a Cause*

"Out here a man settles his own problems."—Tom Doniphon in *The Man Who Shot Liberty Valance*

"Hey, you wanna hear my philosophy of life? Do it to him before he does it to you."—Terry Malloy in *On the Waterfront*

"I'm not dying yet. I have to kill quite a few men first."—Sanjuro Kuwabatake in *Yojimbo*

Personality Weaknesses ★★★★★★★★★★★★★★★★★★★★★★★★★

A Maverick's fiery enthusiasm can sometimes morph into a crazed obsession. They can become so focused on one thing that they forget about everything else in their lives—even eating and sleeping can seem like unnecessary distractions. They become susceptible to their temper, especially when they've neglected to care for themselves for days on end. It's common for Mavericks to lash out at people who are just trying to help. They can also become antisocial, locking themselves away from all people, even the ones they like.

Mavericks struggle with letting people get close to them, including their parents and friends. When they need money, they'll try to tough it out on their own without asking for help. When they go through a bad break-up, they'll hole up in their apartment for days, subsisting only on stale bread and orange juice. When their car breaks down, they'd rather push it single-handedly to the nearest gas station—uphill, in the rain—than call a friend for assistance.

TYPICAL MODES OF TRANSPORTATION

In a cavalcade ★ On horseback ★ Air Force One ★
Pirate ship ★ Motorcycle ★ Hijacked train

CULINARY FAVORITES

Cigarettes ★ Steak and mashed potatoes ★ A sumptuous
Italian meal ★ Anything in a flask ★ Mama's home cookin' ★
Scrambled eggs made by lover

Their Deepest Secret ★★★★★★★★★★★★★★★★★★★★★★★★★★

Mavericks may act as if they don't care what society thinks of them, but in truth, they do care. A lot. A weird look from a stranger will cause them to question everything about themselves. When they meet new people, they commonly feel paranoid, with thoughts like, "Was she looking at my haircut?" or "What's his problem, anyway?" This paranoia often comes from having closed themselves off from others for too long. Although Mavericks may have a tough, unflappable demeanor, their feelings get hurt like everyone else's. They get embarrassed, and they might even blush—they're just good at blushing when no one's looking.

Passionate Mavericks at Work ★★★★★★★★★★★★★★★★★★

Mavericks' behavior at work will vary depending on the circumstance. When they believe in the values of the company they're working for and feel useful to the world at large, they're the hardest workers in the world. They demand that their job contributes to bettering other peoples' lives in some way. But if a job doesn't fit this criterion and a Maverick feels ambivalent about the position he holds, he's prone to quit without notice and float to another job without any outward show of guilt or obligation.

Coworkers tend to see Mavericks as rebellious, smart trendsetters. It's likely that officemates have secret crushes on them. Mavericks may sense this, but they don't let it affect them. If they were to show interest in a coworker, they'd have to reveal their softer side, which means they'd be vulnerable to rejection—and Mavericks avoid making themselves vulnerable at all costs. They'd prefer to take cigarette breaks alone in a stairwell or eat lunch in a remote part of the courtyard.

Bosses envy Mavericks because they gain the kind of respect that bosses want entirely for themselves. Bosses sense the Maverick's rebellious nature and in turn act jumpy around them, fearing the Maverick will lead the other workers in a revolt.

QUINTESSENTIAL BEHAVIOR

Getting tortured for beliefs. ★ Enduring a hunger strike. ★ Blowing up a building in the name of freedom. ★ Participating in a game of chicken—with a tank. ★ Running for public office as a joke. ★ Pirating the high seas. ★ Starting a workers' union. ★ Defending an entire town, all alone.

Passionate Mavericks with Friends ★ ★ ★ ★ ★ ★ ★ ★ ★ ★ ★ ★ ★ ★

Friends see Mavericks as intense, cool, and slightly intimidating. Mavericks can be domineering, especially when it comes to their passions. Friends know that Mavericks who are film buffs are always ready with a movie quote, that Mavericks who are music snobs will know the most obscure and up-and-coming bands, and that Mavericks who are politically minded will have the facts, statistics, and sources to quash any argument.

Mavericks can be counted on to come through in an emergency. When a friend breaks a leg, the Maverick will wait with him in the emergency room. When a Maverick sees a friend in a fight with a stranger, he rushes to her defense no matter what. There's nothing Mavericks enjoy more than taking bad guys down a notch, and they relish the opportunity to do something brave for their friends. They're very protective of the people they care about, although they may only show it in circumstances where they can flex their muscles. Mavericks are not always socially agreeable. At parties, Mavericks will stand in the doorway, assessing whether they should stay or bolt. At boring dinner parties or restaurant outings, a Maverick may sneak outside for a smoke break and never return. Join a Maverick on a double date, and you may find that you're suddenly just a threesome.

MUST-SEE MOVIES FOR
PASSIONATE MAVERICKS

Mavericks delight in watching someone stick it to the Man and fight in the name of the oppressed. They enjoy films that portray the fight for individuality and personal freedom waged by everyday people. Viva la Revolucion!

All the President's Men (1976)

La Battaglia di Algeri (1966)

Bob Roberts (1992)

Fahrenheit 451 (1966)

Five Easy Pieces (1970)

The Great Escape (1963)

High Noon (1952)

Hud (1963)

The Motorcycle Diaries (2004)

On the Waterfront (1954)

Seven Samurai (1954)

Stalingrad (1993)

Taxi Driver (1976)

Passionate Mavericks in Love ★ ★ ★ ★ ★ ★ ★ ★ ★ ★ ★ ★ ★ ★ ★ ★ ★

Mavericks attract lovers who are looking for a "bad boy" or "bad girl"—in other words, they attract suitors everywhere they go. With their devil-may-care approach to life, people think they're incredibly sexy, independent, and ferocious in bed. Mavericks are the leaders of the pack, giving off a vibe of recklessness even though they're in complete control. They'll work this angle, too: They know how to get someone all hot and bothered with a cruel stare, just before abruptly walking out the door.

When entering into a relationship, Mavericks have difficulty letting themselves trust anyone, even when they desperately want to. They will proceed with caution, equipped with all the defenses they have: "I need to focus on my work"; "I've got to get my act together first"; "I'm really busy with my band right now." They'll cut off relationships before they even begin. They tend to be heartbreakers, and their ex-lovers just won't shut up about them.

When Mavericks finally trust someone and fall in love, they unload their passion onto their mates without holding back. Companions love that Mavericks will spontaneously whisk them away to a tropical island, but they hate that Mavericks will feign illness when forced to visit the in-laws. Mavericks do best with someone who is willing to wait out the ups and down of the relationship, knowing that in the end they'll wind up riding on the Maverick's motorcycle into the sunset.

Most Compatible Cinescope Types ★★★★★★★★★★★★★★★★★

 The Rebellious Lover. Mavericks and Lovers are drawn together like magnets. Lovers want mates who challenge society's views, and they gravitate toward forbidden romances. These two want to be noticed, both as a couple and as individuals. They delight in shocked stares from the crowds. They'll make love in taboo settings. They'll play off one another's feistiness and behave like animals in heat. Like Jim Stark (Maverick) and Judy (Lover) in *Rebel Without a Cause*, the intensity of their relationship increases with every moment they spend together.

 Youthful Sages represent the good conscience of Mavericks, and the two are naturally attracted to each other. Sages envy Mavericks' emotional outbursts, while Mavericks appreciate the Sage's ability to remain calm. In a relationship, they balance each other out; if they quarrel fiercely, they make up fiercely, too. In *V for Vendetta*, V (Maverick) and Evey Hammond (Sage) use their relationship to incite a revolution.

Least Compatible Cinescope Type ★★★★★★★★★★★★★★★★★

 The Vivacious Romantic. Mavericks don't like to be cuddly, and Romantics don't like to cut to the chase. If these two were to hook up, the Maverick would sneak out the door the next morning to avoid any sentimentality. Mavericks tend to take Romantics for granted, and Romantics tend to smother Mavericks, unintentionally pushing them away. In *A Place in the Sun*, George Eastman (Rebel) leaves good wife Alice (Romantic) for a steamy affair with Angela Vickers (Lover) . . . and the movie doesn't end well for Alice.

Other Cinescope Types Who Are Rebels with a Cause ★ ★ ★ ★ ★

Like Mavericks, **Magical Creators** and **Dedicated Idealists** push the boundaries of "normal" behavior. These three heroes would spend conversations praising their idols, criticizing politicians, and making fun of small-minded people. Creators and Mavericks share a tendency to challenge society, and as a result, they can understand and love one another. When Mavericks are able to convince Idealists to wave their freak flags high, these two types stand a good chance in love as well.

Other Cinescope Types Who Wear Their Intensity on Their Sleeves ★

Destined Hunters and **Existential Saviors.** When these three heroes are in the same room, the walls might crumble from the tension they emit. In romance, they'd face unbearable stress that would explode in disaster, but in business, these three can work together to solve the world's problems. Using a Hunter's brawn, a Savior's mind, and a Maverick's power, they'd certainly intimidate the competition.

The Passionate Maverick's Greatest Nemesis ★ ★ ★ ★ ★ ★ ★ ★ ★

The Ruthless Tyrant. Tyrants control the machine that Mavericks seek to destroy. Emotionless and cold, Tyrants seek to strip the world of its fire and leave it in a robotic, brainwashed state. Tyrants represent big corporations, big empires, and big suits with big money, and the Maverick is the voice of the meek that they oppress. Ultimately, Ruthless Tyrants will be defeated because they have no souls. When their soulessness is revealed, Mavericks can rally the masses to their cause. In *A Few Good Men*, Col. Jessup is a Tyrant who is taken down unforgettably by Lt. Kaffee (Maverick).

Why do Mavericks hate Tyrants so much? What would happen if a Maverick's ambition to change the world actually came to fruition? They'd be in charge, and the power would go to their heads. From there, it's a short journey to tyranny.

Words of Advice ★

Sometimes, being uncool can be fun. Channel your inner dork once in awhile: Play board games, read a comic book, or embarrass yourself on the dance floor. Unwind and enjoy life more. And don't worry; everyone will think you're the coolest person in the room anyway.

REBELLIOUS LOVER

Glossary Code: RL

The course of true love never did run smooth, but it might just be the only thing in life worth fighting for. Rebellious Lovers can feel constrained in a world where they don't quite belong, and their choice in lovers reflects this. They are driven by their passions—they make bold choices in love, and they live life with a unique flair. They can be very emotional, especially in times of sadness. Lovers long to feel the thrill of the chase; and time and time again, they seek to relive this feeling. Nonetheless, in giving themselves to another person they realize how beautiful life can be. As Rebellious Lover Noah would tell you in *The Notebook*, "I've loved another with all my heart and soul; and to me, this has always been enough."

Famous Rebellious Lovers

- ★ Rose Bukater (*Titanic*)
- ★ Dr. John Prentice (*Guess Who's Coming to Dinner*)
- ★ Juliet (*Romeo and Juliet*)
- ★ Ennis (*Brokeback Mountain*)
- ★ Belle (*Beauty and the Beast*)
- ★ Paul (*Last Tango in Paris*)

Rebellious Lover Typecasting

- ★ Leonardo DiCaprio
- ★ Elizabeth Taylor
- ★ Burt Lancaster
- ★ Marlene Dietrich
- ★ Kate Winslet
- ★ Antonio Banderas

Personality Strengths ★★★★★★★★★★★★★★★★★★★★★★★★★

Rebellious Lovers firmly believe in having love at any cost. They'll always tell you to follow your heart, and they'll lead by example. They certainly don't marry for convenience or for money; in fact, the mere thought of doing so makes them nauseous. They've got ideals, dreams, and hopes for their romantic future, and they're steadfast in their pursuit of them. They're the kinds of people with beautiful stories about falling in love that inspire younger people to go out and do the same. Rebellious Lovers are driven by their passions. They make bold choices in love, and they live life with a unique flair.

Lovers have no problem facing challenges in all aspects of life. If they feel destined to do something, they're going to do it. There's no talking sense into them; when they get an idea, it's already a done deal. Lovers never do anything half-assed: It's all or nothing. This attitude gets them far in love, in life, and in bed.

Lovers are one-of-a-kind individuals. They are endlessly excited about life, and they love to try new things. Hang out with a Lover, and your eyes will certainly be opened.

QUINTESSENTIAL STATEMENTS

"I think you're swell—so long as I'm not your husband."—Walter Neff in *Double Indemnity*

"And so I will hide it away with all things left unsaid and undone between us."—Susannah in *Legends of the Fall*

"There's a place for us . . . hold my hand and I'll take you there . . . somehow . . . someday."—Maria in *West Side Story*

"Only the best people fight against all obstacles in pursuit of happiness."—Juliet Hulme in *Heavenly Creatures*

"Winter must be cold for those with no warm memories . . . And we've already missed the spring!"—Terry McKay in *An Affair to Remember*

"Oh Jerry, don't let's ask for the moon. We have the stars."—Charlotte Vale in *Now, Voyager*

Personality Weaknesses ★★★★★★★★★★★★★★★★★★★★★★

Lovers struggle with moderation. Going balls-to-the-wall may win Lovers a prized kiss, but it could lead to disaster in the long run. They invest so much energy in relationships that they may not always realize when a relationship needs to end. Being stubbornly determined not to look at things from a realistic point of view can lead to getting hurt. When they feel pain, they feel it to an extreme. Expect moping, sobbing fits, and angry journal writing.

When Lovers find a partner in love, they devote their mind, body, and soul to the relationship, but everything else in their life gets put on hold; it's like time has stopped completely. This can have ripple effects on their careers, friendships, and family if they aren't careful.

TYPICAL MODES OF TRANSPORTATION

Mercedes Benz ★ Running through fields in slow motion ★
Back of a police car ★ Strolling through rival gang turf ★
On the front of an ocean liner, with arms spread and eyes closed ★
On the back of a sensually muscular horse

CULINARY FAVORITES

Melted chocolate poured over a lover's body ★ Apples ★
Red wine ★ Gourmet dinner at fancy restaurant ★ Dinner served
in a dimly lit apartment ★ Poison

Their Deepest Secret ★★★★★★★★★★★★★★★★★★★★★★★

Although Lovers preach endlessly to others about love, deep inside they doubt whether they're worthy of it. They may build their whole lives around pursuing it, but in a way, they're also running away from themselves. Despite their constant success with love, Lovers feel insecure about every new affair. They harbor thoughts like: "Do I really deserve this?" and "Why is this person with me?" It would be wise for Lovers to work on themselves before throwing themselves into complex relationships.

Rebellious Lovers at Work ★★★★★★★★★★★★★★★★★★★★

Lovers prefer jobs that feed their passions and interests. They are not bound by the constraints of choosing a job just because it pays well or improves their status. If they do go into the corporate world, you can count on them to use it to help others; pro-bono work is not uncommon.

Coworkers respect Lovers because of their serious approach to getting things accomplished. They care about their jobs and they care about their coworkers. Of course, if they are in the midst of an intense love affair, their minds will be elsewhere. They'll fantasize about their sex lives when they're supposed to be planning a presentation. This is expected from Lovers, and coworkers won't fault them for it. After all, they can't wait to hear the juicy details!

Bosses admire the passion that Lovers bring to work. However, they don't like it when Lovers get emotional on the job. Coworkers will rally around the ailing Lover, and the boss will silently grow irritable.

QUINTESSENTIAL BEHAVIOR

Having sex in a public place. ★ Getting in a gunfight over a woman. ★ Getting in a catfight over a man. ★ Writing a novel about the latest love affair. ★ Helping conspire to murder an ex-lover. ★ Dying saving the life of another. ★ Having an affair with a brother's spouse. ★ Falling in love with a misunderstood monster.

Rebellious Lovers with Friends ★★★★★★★★★★★★★★★★★★★

Lovers enjoy finding out what makes people tick. If someone is different from them on the outside, Lovers will always find common ground. This results in them having friends with a wide array of personalities, from hermits to extroverts. Lovers serve as the social glue that keeps their diverse group of friends together.

Friends admire Lovers for their nonjudgmental approach to life. They're so open-minded that they inspire liberal attitudes in even the most uptight individuals. Lovers often draw attention in social situations because they'll confront people when they need to be confronted. Friends get a kick out of this when it's someone who deserves a comeuppance, but when it's directed at their date, they find it annoying.

Friends can always count on Lovers to share all the sordid details about their last fling but can't always count on them to heed good advice. Friends will endlessly warn Lovers to proceed with caution in love, and Lovers will nod politely . . . and do just the opposite.

Rebellious Lovers in Love ★★★★★★★★★★★★★★★★★★★★★★★★

When a Lover decides to woo you, you're really in for it! You're getting the full treatment: poetry, roses, serenades, and an overwhelming amount of sexual attention. There's really no escape; they're completely determined to get what they want. However, Lovers don't think before they fall. They tend to go with their first instinct, which is not always the best idea. They love so hard that once they begin, they just can't stop.

Lovers come alive when they explore being physical with another person. They are risk-takers in their sex lives and drawn to more unorthodox practices. They don't mind public displays of affection—they crave them. They like to get their kicks in elevators, bleachers, and alleys. The world is their oyster.

In the long-term, Lovers can burn out fast. They can become easily disappointed once reality strikes and clashes with the fantasy they've built. Once their mate falls off the pedestal, a Lover can grow angry and confused. Lovers who fare the best in relationships learn to slow down the pace from the start.

MUST-SEE MOVIES FOR
REBELLIOUS LOVERS

Rebellious Lovers like movies about a rebel who bucks social norms to love someone vastly different from them. Whether it's a matter of class, race, religion, or species, they like their films to portray a fight for love. The endings are almost always tragic, but the triumph of love is highlighted.

Boys Don't Cry (1999)
Breathless (1960)
Carnal Knowledge (1971)
Dangerous Beauty (1998)
Laurel Canyon (2002)

Lolita (1962)
The New World (2005)
Sex, Lies, and Videotape (1989)
Sid and Nancy (1986)

Somewhere in Time (1980)
Splendor in the Grass (1961)
Y Tu Mama Tabien (2001)

Most Compatible Cinescope Types ★★★★★★★★★★★★★★★★★★

The Passionate Maverick. These heroes need each other. Who else shares such intensity about social issues and also lives to break down barriers? To be with anyone else would probably be a complete bore! These heroes feed off their passion for each other and have crazy sexual escapades. In *On the Waterfront*, Terry Malloy (Maverick) needs the undying support of Edie (Lover) in order to challenge authority.

Charismatic Performers can make a good match for Lovers. Performers like their love hot and heavy, and Lovers are just the ones for the job. Lovers like to be entertained and enthralled by mystery; Performers are just the ticket. Both types know how to heat up a romance with seduction. In *Gilda*, Johnny Gambell (Lover) takes a big chance by pursuing Gilda (Performer), and despite her homicidal husband's attempts to stop them, they enjoy a passionate affair.

Least Compatible Cinescope Type ★★★★★★★★★★★★★★★★★★

The Youthful Sage. Lovers are way too emotionally concentrated for sensitive Sages. These two would clash right from the start—Sages are put off by outward seductive aggression, and Lovers are turned off by practical thinking. In *The Graduate*, Mrs. Robinson (Lover) is much too much for young Benjamin Braddock (Sage) . . . but the level-headed daughter will do just fine.

Other Cinescope Types Who Feel Comfortable with Their Sexuality ★★★★★★★★★★★★★★★★★★★★★★★★★★★★★★

Like Lovers, **Destined Hunters** and **Respected Champions** use their sexuality to their greatest advantage. All three crave physical attention, and they know how to work it. If you were being seduced by these three heroes, there would be no hope for your getting out alive. As friends, they would clash and steal each other's dates. As lovers, they wouldn't do much better. Their overt sensuality would spark paranoia and lead to jealousy.

Other Cinescope Types Who Like to Be Unconventional ★★★★

Magical Creators and **Existential Saviors** tend to be untraditional in their approach to life, just like Lovers. All three would hate to be called "normal"; they associate that word with "boring." These types might have passionate flings that would end almost as soon as they began. Lovers would find Creators too silly and Saviors too philosophical to fuel their adrenaline. However, they are all fascinated by unusual behavior and events, and they might all enjoy reading the "Oddly Enough" news section online.

The Rebellious Lover's Greatest Nemesis ★★★★★★★★★★★★

 The Spiteful Rival. Rivals pursue the same objects of desire that Lovers do. Rivals are petty, small-minded, and condescending. They make Lovers feel like unwanted outcasts. Ultimately, Rivals become predictable in their spiteful tactics, and their true colors shine through to the person they're trying to impress, as in *Titanic*, when Cal (Rival) does everything possible to stop Jack (Lover) from getting Rose.

Why do Rivals irritate Lovers so much? Underneath it all, both types are uncertain about whether they're truly worthy of love. They aggressively combat each other instead of dealing with their own fears. If Lovers feel defeated, they might act as spiteful and hostile as the Rival they're competing against.

Advice for Rebellious Lovers ★★★★★★★★★★★★★★★★★★★

Try a group activity to keep yourself grounded in a world outside of relationships. Join a book club, a bowling league, or a poker night. Hanging out in a group on a regular basis will bring some stability to your life. Besides, it's good to have friends around when a love affair goes south.

RESPECTED CHAMPION

#1

Glossary Code: RC

Nobody understands the struggle of the underdog better than Respected Champions. They have big dreams, big hearts, and big ambitions that drive them. Champions aren't all athletes, but they possess a natural winning attitude that attracts many fans. They're at their best when they're making others feel included in a social situation and working a room. They're naturally popular because of their unyielding ambition, but their intense hunger for victory can land them in trouble when they take loved ones for granted and accidentally hurt someone dear to them in the heat of the moment. But ultimately these heroes always win forgiveness and defeat their adversaries. Mickey says it when he declares in *Rocky*, "You're gonna eat lightnin' and you're gonna crap thunder!!"

Famous Respected Champions

★ Eric "Otter" Stratton in *Animal House*
★ Rocky Balboa in the *Rocky* series
★ Jess Bhamra in *Bend It Like Beckham*
★ Lane Meyer in *Better Off Dead*
★ Torrance Shipman in *Bring It On*
★ Billy Madison in *Billy Madison*

Respected Champion Typecasting

★ Sylvester Stallone
★ Adam Sandler
★ Geena Davis
★ Jack Black
★ Kirsten Dunst
★ Robert Redford

Personality Strengths ★★★★★★★★★★★★★★★★★★★★★★★★

Champions make a point to include everyone in their lives. They like to befriend both men and women, young and old. Whether they're playing baseball with kids or canasta with grandpa, they always feel comfortable. They'll stick their necks out to defend someone who is being picked on, even if they personally can't stand the victim. They'll invite the odd man out to a group event every time. In school, they were the kids who protected the nerds from getting their milk money stolen.

Champions are very popular people. They attract a lot of attention due to their sense of humor, which can level all playing fields. So what if you've got two degrees from Harvard? In a battle of wits against a Champion, you're going down in flames. They are brimming with a solid sense of self that doesn't waver. When a Champion really shines, they can brighten up even the grimmest situation.

These heroes have a strict moral code and strive very hard to always do the right thing. If they feel as if they've offended a friend or let someone down, it will eat away at them endlessly. They won't be able to go about their day until they've made a bad thing good.

QUINTESSENTIAL STATEMENTS

"The Price is wrong . . . bitch."—Happy Gilmore in *Happy Gilmore*

"They're not gonna catch us. We're on a mission from God."—Elwood in *Blues Brothers*

"All right, let's show 'em what we got, guys! Get out there on the ice and let 'em know you're there." —Reggie Dunlop in *Slap Shot*

"There's nothing I can't do with a racecar."—Cole Trickle in *Days of Thunder*

"But you know what, they forgot something: I have to win."—Steve Prefontaine in *Prefontaine*

"Girls only want boyfriends who have great skills."—Napoleon in *Napoleon Dynamite*

Personality Weaknesses ★★★★★★★★★★★★★★★★★★★★★★★

Champions love to have fun at any cost but have trouble facing reality. When faced with a downer task, Champions avoid it for days on end. If they crash the car by accident, their solution might be, "Let's throw a toga party!" Sometimes this irrational behavior can lead to bigger problems down the road.

Champions desperately need to feel victorious. When they feel the least bit threatened, they become grouchy and guarded. They lash out so severely that their words sound spiteful. If you're playing a sport with a Champion and piss them off, they'll probably wind up penalized for bad behavior. If they don't succeed at something, whether it's school, work, or relationships, they feel completely defeated, despite their many past victories.

TYPICAL MODES OF TRANSPORTATION

Old car transformed into a parade float ★ Golf cart ★ Jogging ★
Ten-speed bicycles ★ Running naked through suburban streets ★
Running fully clothed through urban streets

CULINARY FAVORITES

As much food as can be stuffed into one's mouth ★ Victory champagne ★
Raw egg protein shakes ★ Jello shots ★ Hamburger ★ Beer, and lots of it

Their Deepest Secret ★★★★★★★★★★★★★★★★★★★★★★★

While Champions appear to be buzzing with confidence, deep down they're not as sure of themselves as they appear to be. They're full of doubts about whether or not they can pull off even the smallest task. Every so often, they withdraw into solitary confinement just to get a grip on how to make their next move. Although a Champion can rally support from the masses, oftentimes this feels like a task they don't want to be burdened with. They take on everyone's problems, and as a result, they tend to feel an enormous amount of pressure to succeed. Learning to relax and take many breaks throughout the day is essential to their well-being.

Respected Champions at Work ★★★★★★★★★★★★★★★★★★

In the workplace, Champions are masters of their domain. People adore them, have loving nicknames for them, and desperately want to befriend or date them. They'll receive cryptic notes on Post-Its from random people. They'll get invited to parties by coworkers they can't remember. They'll receive praise from people they didn't even know worked in the building.

Champions strive to be good at everything they take on, and this is certainly true for them at work. They're exceedingly honest and virtuous; they'd never steal from petty cash or report hours they didn't work. Even in front of a full conference room, they'll defend coworkers who are getting picked on. They rarely think twice about doing the right thing. Champions tend to have the social prowess that bosses want all for themselves. Once in a while, Champions might say something stinging to upper management if they feel it's justified. This makes bosses antsy—they never know what they're going to get.

QUINTESSENTIAL BEHAVIOR

Throwing a keg party as an act of resistance. ★ Playing golf with a hockey stick. ★ Branding one's own ass to get a laugh. ★ Planting hidden video cameras in a sorority house. ★ Chugging beer to forget about troubles. ★ Disrupting posh functions with obnoxious behavior. ★ Chugging beer to relive one's youth. ★ Using a trick maneuver to win a championship. ★ Competing in a spontaneous dance-off.

Respected Champions with Friends ★★★★★★★★★★★★★★★★

Champions have many friends, and they struggle to keep track of most of them. Befriending people is as natural as breathing for them. If they're out drinking, they'll get to know the entire bar. If they're dating someone, they'll soon be on a first-name basis with the entire family. They like to include people, because they love to be surrounded by big groups.

Friends see Champions as charismatic, popular, and, at times, a little too carefree. This casual approach to life can end in mishaps; credit cards will be maxed out, cars will get towed, hook-ups will be regretted. Friends love that Champions include everyone but hate that Champions lack the discipline to control the chaos that ensues.

Friends can always count on Champions to be the life of the party. Champions are truly in their element leading a group to debauchery and good times. However, friends can't always count on Champions to conform to situations that may require it. Trying to change a Champion's personality is futile and should not be attempted. "I am what I am" is the credo of Champions everywhere.

Respected Champions in Love ★★★★★★★★★★★★★★★★★★

Champions excel at the game of love—it's just another game, after all. They know how to play it, work it, and win it. They wear their winning attitude on their sleeves and go out of their way to show their kindness to strangers. These charming qualities attract many potential lovers of all types.

However, being good at an easy game is distasteful to a Champion. They like to make it difficult. They'll pick the one person in the room who isn't interested and pursue them with all the gusto that they've got. Often, they'll pick someone who's an awful match for them and spend endless amounts of time trying to justify the relationship. As a result, long-term relationships can be hard; Champions only know how to land their date, not stay with them for the entire season.

Champions will eventually learn to make better decisions in the beginning and, therefore, have greater success in the long term. If they can find companions who love their natural strength and sarcastic wit, they'll find that sticking with their partner is a no-brainer. Champions make exciting life partners, and their drive toward success fuels their love.

MUST-SEE MOVIES FOR
RESPECTED CHAMPIONS

Respected Champions like movie heroes who are sweet-natured but fierce on the playing field. They may face cheating competitors and incredible odds, but with the help of their friends, these heroes always come out on top.

The Bad News Bears (1976)	*Enter the Dragon* (1973)	*Revenge of the Nerds* (1984)
Blades of Glory (2007)	*Midnight Madness* (1980)	*Rollerball* (1975)
Breakin' 2: Electric Boogaloo (1984)	*Moving Violations* (1985)	*Rounders* (1998)
	Nacho Libre (2006)	*War of the Roses* (1989)
	Real Genius (1985)	

Most Compatible Cinescope Types ★★★★★★★★★★★★★★

 The Invincible Optimist. Like Champions, Optimists have the kind of contagious humor that gets everyone rolling on the floor. Together, they make a formidable comedic duo that no one could ever stop. They have each other in stitches before they even make it through the first date. Like Blutarski (Optimist) and Otter (Champion) in *Animal House*, they might have their low points, but they're too busy laughing to notice.

 Vivacious Romantics tend to fall fast and hard for Champions. Both are full of energy and charm; they flirt with each other endlessly. These two tend to have an elaborate and drawn-out wooing period that subsequently leads to some action. Like Adrien (Romantic) and Rocky Balboa (Champion) in *Rocky*, their relationship might take a beating, but eventually he will admit he loves her.

Least Compatible Cinescope Type ★★★★★★★★★★★★★★★★★

 The Dedicated Idealist. While these heroes both strive for success, they have drastically different views on how to attain it. Idealists focus on hard labor while Champions focus on making bold moves. Idealists tend to resent Champions for their carefree attitude, and Champions tend to resent Idealists for their harsh work ethic. In love, they bicker. In *The Color of Money*, Vincent (Champion) and Eddie (Idealist) clash in their approach to getting ahead in life.

Other Cinescope Types Who Take Competition Seriously ★★★

 Along with Champions, **Destined Hunters** and **Charismatic Performers** tend to get caught up in competition. Whether it's winning a Halloween costume contest or watching *Jeopardy!* with friends, they aim to win. In love, these competitive tendencies conflict. On the same team, they would enjoy each other's enthusiasm for winning. On opposing teams, they just might let things get too personal. Ever see a Monopoly board get flipped over? Hang out with these heroes, and beware of the flying thimble!

Other Cinescope Types Who Like to Party ★★★★★★★★★★★

 Like Champions, **Magical Creators** and **Loyal Warriors** like to let their hair down and get a little wild. Champions and Warriors tend to party in traditional ways—clubs, concerts, and sporting events. As a result, they're often the very best of friends. Creators are more unorthodox, but open-minded Champions can get down with this. As friends, Creators and Champions have fun behaving badly together. As lovers, Warriors and Champions stand a great chance and probably will wind up kissing on the big-screen at a game.

The Respected Champion's Greatest Nemesis ★ ★ ★ ★ ★ ★ ★ ★ ★

 The Taunting Bully. Bullies seek to torture those who are weaker than they are with menacing words and physical force. They like to pick on Champions because they feel threatened by them. Bullies are endlessly annoying but also easy to beat; in the end, they're easily crushed by the natural confidence of their rival. In *Cinderella Man*, Max Baer (Bully) taunts Jim Braddock (Champion), only fueling Jim's desire for victory.

Why do Champions wan to beat Bullies so badly? If Champions get too caught up in trying to succeed, their trash-talking could turn into blatant disrespect for others. Taunting Bullies are what Champions could become if they let their egos get out of control.

Advice for Respected Champions ★ ★ ★ ★ ★ ★ ★ ★ ★ ★ ★ ★ ★ ★ ★

Plan a time each week to take care of all your boring errands at once. Having a schedule that's consistent is crucial; it's easy to procrastinate otherwise. You'll find it takes only an hour to finish everything instead of the ten hours of avoidance you've grown used to. After all, that valuable time could be spent partying!

VIVACIOUS ROMANTIC

Glossary Code: VR

Vivacious Romantics have big, warm hearts, and their dreams of true love are enduring. They're close with their families, loyal to their friends, and probably love their pets a little too much. Whether they know it or not, they are on a mission to find "The One"—the person they believe will complete them. This can cause them to change their personalities to attract an "ideal" mate—and can lead to drunken voicemails and embarrassing misunderstandings. But once Vivacious Romantics realize that true romance hinges on the desire to understand and to be understood, they can confidently reveal their real selves to the world and open themselves to love. As Vivacious Romantic Westley said in *The Princess Bride*, "This is true love . . . you think this happens every day?"

Famous Vivacious Romantics

★ Robbie Hart in *The Wedding Singer*
★ Ellie Andrews in *It Happened One Night*
★ Harry Burns in *When Harry Met Sally*
★ Tracy Lord in *The Philadelphia Story*
★ William Thacker in *Notting Hill*
★ Annie Reed in *Sleepless in Seattle*

Vivacious Romantic Typecasting

★ Meg Ryan
★ Colin Firth
★ Drew Barrymore
★ Taye Diggs
★ Cary Grant
★ Katharine Hepburn

Personality Strengths ★★★★★★★★★★★★★★★★★★★★★★★★★★★★★★

Vivacious Romantics are delightful and expressive people. They have an abundance of friends and potential suitors, due in large part to their unique ability to see beauty everywhere they look. See that amazing bridge? Check out that gorgeous sunset! Look at all those wonderful commuters! Romantics have a spirit that allows them to seize the essence of every happy moment and remember it forever. When you're around a Romantic, you can't help but feel as if you're floating on cloud nine.

Romantics are ruled by their hearts in their approach to life and relationships. Some might even call them "bleeding hearts." They are sincere in their compassion, and they act on it without remorse—taking a wounded pigeon to the vet while on the way to work would be more important than making it to the office on time.

Romantics are the masters of witty banter. Put them in any situation and they'll talk their way into a better one without even trying. This skill certainly comes in handy in job interviews or while haggling over prices at the dry cleaners. Romantics are skilled at flirtatious repartee, leaving their counterparts tongue-tied. This kind of natural spunk allows Romantics to chase their dreams with unbridled enthusiasm.

QUINTESSENTIAL STATEMENTS

"It's really human of you to listen to all my bullshit."—Samantha in *Sixteen Candles*

"I'm a bagel on a plate full of onion rolls!"—Fannie Brice in *Funny Girl*

"I am determined that nothing but the deepest love could ever induce me into matrimony."—Elizabeth Bennet in *Pride & Prejudice*

"Love is too weak a word for what I feel . . . I luuurve you, you know, I loave you, I luff you."—Alvy Singer in *Annie Hall*

"It seems to me that love is everywhere. Often it's not particularly dignified or newsworthy, but it's always there."—The Prime Minister in *Love Actually*

"She's gone. She gave me a pen. I gave her my heart—she gave me a pen."—Lloyd Dobler in *Say Anything*

Personality Weaknesses ★★★★★★★★★★★★★★★★★★★★★★★

Romantics put excessive pressure on themselves, especially when it comes to love. They value love above all else, and they can spend so much energy pursuing it that they actually wind up working against their own interests. They'll try to do all the "right" things—they wear stylish clothes, work out obsessively, and visit the trendiest bars, even when all they really want to do is to lounge at home in their pajamas with a tub of ice cream. They may even be overly accommodating with an ex-lover—"Sure, I'll help you move!" In other words, they try very hard to be the person they think they should be, and potential mates are confused by their phoniness.

A Romantic's insecurity can result in neurotic actions. When self-doubt kicks in, these heroes plunge into anxious inner monologues that lead to quirky social behavior. They'll walk into glass doors, trip over dessert trays, or accidentally insult a sexy coworker in mid-seduction. These gaffes can lead to outright panic and overreaction, another behavior commonly displayed by Romantics: "I can't believe I just said that! I guess I have to quit my job now!"

TYPICAL MODES OF TRANSPORTATION

Horse-drawn carriage through Central Park ★ Running after a
dream lover ★ Skipping down a crowded avenue ★ Dancing in
the rain ★ Carried across the threshold of a new home

CULINARY FAVORITES

Shared plate of spaghetti ★ Entire bottle of wine ★ Box of chocolates
from admirer ★ Frozen dinner in front of TV ★ Entire pint of
ice cream ★ Candlelit dinner on rooftop

Their Deepest Secret ★★★★★★★★★★★★★★★★★★★★★★★★★

Vivacious Romantics appear to be entirely focused on finding the love of their life, but in reality, they just want to find themselves. They sometimes feel out of touch with their own identity, and though they have many admirers who recognize the best in them, they have a hard time admiring their own amazing qualities. Deep down, they know that understanding themselves is their true quest in life, despite their outward journey to find a romantic counterpart. All Romantics quietly understand that it's hard to truly love another if you don't love yourself first.

Vivacious Romantics at Work ★ ★ ★ ★ ★ ★ ★ ★ ★ ★ ★ ★ ★ ★ ★ ★ ★ ★ ★

In the workplace, Romantics are full of giddy energy. They maintain a pleasant attitude even when they hate their job or loathe their boss. Romantics take great pride in the positive influence their liveliness has on the office. They like to sneak gossip breaks with coworkers, and they're the first ones to spread the word when a hot new temp is hired.

Coworkers love Romantics because they're easy to get along with. Romantics tend to go with the flow, and unless their relationship is going badly, they tend to remain upbeat. If they genuinely like the people they work with, Romantics can stay in the same job for years.

Bosses tend to have a generally positive impression of Romantics, thinking of them as friendly and happy. However, the Romantic's tendency to daydream can come across as absentmindedness to the boss. And if a Romantic finds a boss physically attractive, watch out! Hot coffee will be spilled, revealing emails will accidentally be forwarded to the entire office, and ridiculous antics are sure to ensue.

QUINTESSENTIAL BEHAVIOR

Insulting a lover and feeling awful about it later. ★ Dancing in the middle of a crowded street. ★ Avoiding eye-contact on an elevator. ★ Chasing a lover through an airport terminal. ★ Splashing around in a public fountain. ★ Throwing roses in the trash only to retrieve them a few seconds later. ★ Saying all the wrong things at the right times. ★ Saying all the right things at the wrong times. ★ Saying all the right things at the right times when the right person finally comes along.

Vivacious Romantics with Friends ★ ★ ★ ★ ★ ★ ★ ★ ★ ★ ★ ★ ★ ★ ★

Romantics are always surrounded by close friends and casual admirers. They can make friends for life, and often keep in touch with childhood pals. Romantics have a special affection for those who share their sentimental habits of saving old love letters and keepsakes.

Friends tend to see Romantics as energetic, caring, and a little exhausting. Catch a Romantic on a good day, and the world is buzzing with energy. Catch a Romantic on a bad day, and you'll get caught up in neuroses. They may tell you the same story about their ex-lover so many times that you'll want to scream, "Enough already!"

Friends can count on Romantics to provide support when it matters most. They care deeply for their friends and will go out of their way to help them. However, when Romantics fall in love, they tend to become distant toward their friends for a little while. Long-term friends who've experienced the ups and downs of the Romantics' attention cycle will understand that they'll be back in regular contact when the new relationship hits a lull.

MUST-SEE MOVIES FOR
VIVACIOUS ROMANTICS

Vivacious Romantics like to watch movies in which a seemingly hopeless case finds a perfect counterpart, particularly in a dramatic climax that involves a sudden and spontaneous proclamation of love. These movies are generally lighthearted and witty, and they revel in the triumph of true love.

Before Sunrise (1994)
Eat Drink Man Woman (1994)
The Goodbye Girl (1974)
Groundhog Day (1993)

High Fidelity (2000)
Jules et Jim (1962)
Midnight (1939)
Muriel's Wedding (1994)
The Purple Rose of Cairo (1985)

Same Time Next Year (1978)
Sliding Doors (1998)
Swingers (1996)

Vivacious Romantics in Love ★ ★ ★ ★ ★ ★ ★ ★ ★ ★ ★ ★ ★ ★ ★ ★ ★ ★ ★

Romantics fall fast and hard; it's just their nature. When they get excited, they get really excited, and there's no holding them back. In long-term relationships, Romantics do well when they find someone who can keep them from feeling insecure.

Though gifts of roses and candy are considered sentimental favorites, Romantics tend to prefer presents that come directly from the heart (not that they'd pass up the roses or candy). A thoughtful card or a nice phone message will go miles with a Romantic, and they'll savor every word. If they have a wonderful date, they'll be appreciative and feel truly happy afterward.

Romantics are often drawn to the wrong types of lovers. It is not uncommon for a Romantic to desperately crave the attention of a loner, such as a Passionate Maverick, and be disappointed with the results. Romantics have a stubborn streak, and they won't abandon a hopeless cause even if it means maintaining a bad relationship. But Romantics are made for true love—once they find it, they know how to make it last.

Most Compatible Cinescope Types ★★★★★★★★★★★★★★★★★

The Respected Champion. Champions and Romantics are both well-liked heroes who draw a lot of attention. Champions possess a confident strength and provide the steady companionship that can stabilize Romantics when they start to get jumpy. The bond between *Bull Durham*'s Annie Savoy (Romantic) and Crash Davis (Champion) exemplifies the best of this type of relationship.

Romantics also get along well with **Dedicated Idealists**, who need romance to fuel their passion to achieve their goals. Both of these personality types have big dreams they're determined to accomplish no matter what gets in the way. When Peter (Idealist) and Joanna (Romantic) support one another in *Office Space*, they realize their goals much faster than they would have alone. Sometimes, all an Idealist needs is a Romantic to cheer him on.

Least Compatible Cinescope Type ★★★★★★★★★★★★★★★★★

The Destined Hunter. Romantics may fantasize about Hunters whisking them away, but in reality, this arrangement never works for long. While Hunters do crave a hug once in awhile, Romantics crave them all the time. The Romantic's need for affection drives a Hunter crazy! In *True Lies*, Harry (Hunter) and Helen (Romantic) have trouble with their marriage until Romantic Helen turns herself into a Hunter—an unlikely scenario in real life.

Other Cinescope Types Who Love Hard and Fast ★★★★★★★★

Determined Survivors and **Rebellious Lovers** are both similar to Romantics because they're guided by their hearts. All three are driven by a desire to bond with other people. In friendship, all three types fully support one another. In relationships, a Lover craves intense forbidden passion, while a Romantic just wants someone cute to snuggle. Survivors and Romantics would spend a lot of time talking on the phone together; their relationship could survive a long-distance scenario.

Other Cinescope Types Who Enjoy Being Delirious ★★★★★★

Magical Creators and **Charismatic Performers** are similar to Romantics in that they love feeling overwhelmed with happiness. Each of these types has a substantial amount of creativity and a real need for external stimulation. As friends, these three would enjoy many mad capers together—for example, they might rent a stretch limo, hang out the sunroof, and holler crazy comments at pedestrians. A love match is more likely to result in a crazy fling than a meaningful, lasting romance.

The Vivacious Romantic's Greatest Nemesis ★★★★★★★★★

The Bitter Buzzkill. Whether in the form of a cynical friend, a bad advice giver, or a competitor, Bitter Buzzkills believe true love doesn't exist. They can quash any spark of romance by injecting a cruel dose of reality into every situation. Buzzkills are most effective when Romantics are feeling low and vulnerable, but when Romantics regain their strength they can easily counter the Buzzkill's naysaying through their own dogged pursuit of love. In *The Wedding Crashers*, Sack Lodge plays Buzzkill to John Beckwith's Romantic as Beckwith tries to win the affections of the beautiful Claire Cleary.

Why do Romantics hate Buzzkills so much? A Buzzkill is just a Romantic with a permanently broken heart, and Romantics desperately fear that the same thing will happen to them. When Romantics feel deflated, they might want to give up on love, too—turning them into the Bitter Buzzkill they loathe.

Words of Advice ★★★★★★★★★★★★★★★★★★★★★★★★★★★

Pour your heart out into a journal on a daily basis. Recording your feelings will give you a wonderful sense of relief. Over time, you'll also gain insight into your own motivations as you reread old entries. Besides, purging on paper is preferable to purging on an ex-lover's answering machine after having a few drinks.

YOUTHFUL SAGE

Glossary Code: YS

Youthful Sages have an irrepressible urge to erupt into spontaneous action when frustration and anger take over. Some of their happier moments were spent as children, and they view adulthood as a bit of a drag. They long for the days when they had less responsibility and greater freedom to explore uncharted areas of life. Youthful Sages tend to have a youthful appearance, whether it's a twinkle of the eye, a bright smile, or a lively energy. Sages know that true contentment can be attained through embracing the experience of being alive. As Ferris Bueller says in *Ferris Bueller's Day Off*, "Life moves pretty fast. If you don't stop and look around once in awhile . . . you could miss it."

Famous Youthful Sages

★ Max Fischer in *Rushmore*
★ Hermione Granger in the *Harry Potter* series
★ Ferris Bueller in *Ferris Bueller's Day Off*
★ Chihiro in *Spirited Away*
★ Cole Sear in *The Sixth Sense*
★ Fern in *Charlotte's Web*

Youthful Sage Typecasting

★ Matthew Broderick
★ Elijah Wood
★ Natalie Portman
★ Dakota Fanning
★ Jason Schwartzman
★ Christina Ricci

Personality Strengths ★★★★★★★★★★★★★★★★★★★★★★★★★

Youthful Sages are full of the instinctive wisdom that others can only wish for. They have the ability to look into both past and present with untarnished clarity, allowing them to see all the potential outcomes their actions may bring in the future. They have a nose for liars—their intuition helps them spot sinister people so they can avoid being taken advantage of.

A Sage's life may encounter some rough times, but through the difficulty they become self-sufficient and fearlessly independent, rarely needing others for support. They can take care of themselves even in the darkest times. If someone breaks their heart, they'll be back at work on Monday. Sages take tremendous pride in being level-headed, sensible, and practical—a Sage may sit and read a book while everyone else is panicking.

Sages are wonderfully empathic people. Political issues often make them fiery with passion, and they tend to take on causes that help people who can't help themselves. When someone is hurt or ailing, they want to offer comfort. If someone's sick, they'll bring chicken soup. If someone is sad, they'll offer a tissue box. Sages extend this concern to the world in general—if they could offer the entire world chicken soup and a tissue box, they would.

QUINTESSENTIAL STATEMENTS

"If you look the right way, you can see that the whole world is a garden."
—Mary in *The Secret Garden*

"Suddenly I realized—two people isn't enough. You need backup. If you're only two people, and someone drops off the edge, then you're on your own. Two isn't a large enough number. You need three at least."
—Marcus Brewer in *About a Boy*

"This is so bad it's gone past good and back to bad again."—Enid in *Ghost World*

"I never had any friends later on like the ones I had when I was twelve. Jesus, does anyone?"—The Writer in *Stand by Me*

"All the great themes have been used up—turned into theme parks."—Mark Hunter in *Pump Up the Volume*

"It would be so nice if something would make sense for a change."
—Alice in *Alice in Wonderland*

Personality Weaknesses ★★★★★★★★★★★★★★★★★★★★★★★

Along with their youthful zeal comes naïveté. Inexperienced with the temptations of the world, Sages are ill prepared when their animal instincts suddenly take over. Sexuality, love, jealousy, and rage are uncommon feelings for them, and they don't navigate these waters gracefully. Though they can take most things in stride, occasionally an unexpected comment will throw a Sage into a wild flurry of conflicting emotions. In this state, Sages can become wild and distempered, unleashing the angst they typically subdue. The best strategy for dealing with these occasional outbursts is to ignore them. Sages prefer to silently forget about such momentary lapses of reason.

Sages do not like to cry. They will go to great lengths to avoid shedding tears, especially in front of others. This is a weakness for them; holding in their tears prevents them from processing their sadness properly. They get so used to exacting control over themselves that when they are in great need of emotional release they sometimes have to strain to cry. But once in a while, perhaps when it is least expected, Sages will let loose a flood of tears they've dammed up for years—in private, of course.

TYPICAL MODES OF TRANSPORTATION

Bicycle ★ Borrowed Ferrari ★ Just walking, lost in thought ★
Show horse ★ Magical flying dog ★ Magical furry cat-bus

CULINARY FAVORITES

Bag of popcorn ★ Ovaltine ★ Reese's Pieces ★ Oddly flavored
jelly beans ★ Porridge ★ Scraps

Their Deepest Secret ★★★★★★★★★★★★★★★★★★★★★★★

While they act like adults, Sages really just want to be kids. They want to be taken care of, held, and comforted. They want to play and have fun without the burden of being articulate and level-headed. They'd like to fail, to be naughty and make mistakes, but they can't seem to allow themselves this luxury. In the end, they opt to remain in control, but there is a part of them that wouldn't mind exploring the depths of their personality once in a while.

Youthful Sages at Work ★

Sages are extremely responsible at work, but they tend to have a strong distaste for the office environment. The workplace is an adult creation, and Sages feel somewhat uncomfortable there. They're squirming in their grown-up shoes and starched collars—they can't wait to go home and change into comfy clothes. Sages tend to be overachievers who crave the respect of others. It makes them uneasy to just maintain the status quo; they feel the need to push themselves to do better all the time.

Coworkers see Sages as reliable, intelligent, and ambitious. Sages are always pitching in, making them well-liked among their peers. They can easily provide the answer to any practical question: how to finish a report, how to spell a word like *onomatopoeia*, and how to figure out the tip on a lunch bill.

Sages just can't shake their deep need for appreciation from their superiors. Thankfully, bosses usually give them respect without restraint. A sinister boss may try to manipulate an eager-to-please Sage by giving her twice the work as a regular employee, knowing that though the Sage may resent the imposition she will do the work anyway.

QUINTESSENTIAL BEHAVIOR

Outsmarting a teacher. ★ Falling in love with someone twice your age. ★ Feeding candy to an alien. ★ Helping a ghost. ★ Playing hooky without getting caught. ★ Convincing crazed gangs not to rumble. ★ Giving a moving, tear-jerking speech. ★ Running for class president.

Youthful Sages with Friends ★ ★ ★ ★ ★ ★ ★ ★ ★ ★ ★ ★ ★ ★ ★ ★ ★ ★ ★

Sages are mild mannered and pleasant in social activities with friends. In group activities, Sages tend to hang back and let everyone else do their thing. They're usually reserved in conversation until talk turns to a subject about which they are passionately opinionated. Then just try to shut them up!

Friends think of Sages as open-minded, inquisitive, and well-mannered. Sages are great at parties, as they can jump in and out of stimulating conversations while remaining polite to everyone around them. Their independence makes them agreeable additions to most social outings.

Friends know to avoid angering a Sage. While Sages are usually collected and patient, when provoked a Sage will harbor lasting ill-will. Cross the line and a Sage may never speak to you again, or he may resent you silently for years. Either way, he'll let his rage be known—albeit in a clearly mature and responsible manner.

Youthful Sages in Love ★★★★★★★★★★★★★★★★★★★★★★★★

Sages flirt with the idea of love just like they flirt with their suitors. They entice their potential lovers with their intellectual confidence while confusing them with their emotional indecisiveness. This often results in a push/pull dynamic that leaves Sages (and suitors!) frustrated.

Sages possess firm ideals, which is an attribute suitors perceive as both intimidating and seductive. However, Sages rarely use their sexuality to their best advantage; they tend to skirt around the issue of sex. When faced with an aggressive suitor, a Sage will want to run and hide.

Sages make wonderful and inspiring long-term companions. They dislike the chase, but they thrive in a steady relationship with someone who truly appreciates their sensitive nature. It is essential for Sages to find a mate who can connect with their fun side. When a relationship clicks, it is full of sentimental sleigh rides, skipping through parks, holding hands in the rain, and beautiful moments that Sages daydream about.

MUST-SEE MOVIES FOR
YOUTHFUL SAGES

Youthful Sages enjoy movies that idealize the childhood experience. Ultimately, their movies tend to share a message about teaching empathy and sensitivity to a jaded world.

A Christmas Story (1983)
City of God (2002)
The City of Lost Children (1995)
Election (1999)
400 Blows (1959)

A Guide to Recognizing Your Saints (1996)
Ladri di Biciclette (1948)
Léolo (1992)
My Life as a Dog (1985)
A Little Princess (1995)

My Neighbor Totoro (1988)
Over the Edge (1979)
Paper Moon (1973)

Most Compatible Cinescope Types ★★★★★★★★★★★★★★★

The Chosen Adventurer. Sages and Adventurers make great partners in life. Adventurers help Sages go out and experience the adult side of the world. In return, Sages give Adventurers their undying trust and loyalty. Sages can also help to bring out an Adventurer's sentimental side, as in the relationship between Billy (Sage) and Basie (Adventurer) in *Empire of the Sun*.

The Magical Creator. Sages tend to be old souls, while Magical Creators tend to be young souls—but somewhere in the middle, these two get along famously. Creators fulfill Sages' fantasies of acting like crazy kids, and Sages can help Creators by grounding their eccentric ideas in reality. In the end, it's their mutual love of magic that keeps the two together for wild capers like the ones shared by Willy Wonka (Creator) and Charlie (Sage) in *Charlie and the Chocolate Factory*.

Least Compatible Cinescope Type ★★★★★★★★★★★★★★★

The Courageous Detective. Detectives lack the innocence that makes Youthful Sages really shine. Detectives live in a strictly adult world, and Sages prefer to avoid that world. Although both personality types are disciplined, their spiritual views conflict. In *E.T.*, Elliott (Sage) attempts to protect his alien friend from Keys (Detective), who doesn't fully grasp the mysticism of the situation.

Other Cinescope Types Who Speak Sensibly ★★★★★★★★★

Dedicated Idealists and **Respected Champions** share the Sage's tendency to inject a needed dose of reality in out-of-control situations. Before anyone else realizes that the building is on fire, an Idealist will be motioning to the door. When the red light appears on your dashboard because your gas tank is empty, a Champion will point it out. When the world seems to have gone mad, a Sage will shed light on the cause. These three personalities tend to befriend one another, make each other laugh, and flirt endlessly—but when they try pairing off into couples, their relationships never get off the ground.

Other Cinescope Types Who Are Compassionate to People in Need ★★★★★★★★★★★★★★★★★★★★★★★★★★★★

Enlightened Healers and **Passionate Mavericks** are like Sages in their empathy for those in pain; all three have the instinct to save others from their ills. But though they share this impulse, they approach the situation differently: Mavericks are aggressive, Healers are empathetic, and Sages are rational. As relationships go, these three types would probably rather volunteer at soup kitchens together than hook up. However, Healers and Sages stand a good chance in marriage because of their similar sensitive styles.

The Youthful Sage's Greatest Nemesis ★★★★★★★★★★★★★

The Heartless Curmudgeon. Whether they're demented parents, cruel teachers, or cranky cynics, Curmudgeons always represent the nightmarish world of adults. To these villains, compassion and sensitivity are flaws, and greed and fear are promoted as strengths. But Curmudgeons are creatures of habit—Sages can take advantage of their predictability to gain the upper hand. In *The Goonies*, a pack of Sages must face off with Mama Fratelli, the definitive cranky Curmudgeon.

Sages and Curmudgeons share the tendency to shut out unwelcome feelings. Sages can sometimes act too old for their age, robbing themselves of any fun, and behave just like the villains they loathe.

Words of Advice ★★★★★★★★★★★★★★★★★★★★★★★★★★★

Unleash your inner angst by watching dramatic movies such as *Shadowlands*, *An Affair to Remember*, or *Million Dollar Baby*. By reconnecting with painful emotions you've suppressed, you'll feel a sense of closure over past events.

THE
MOVIE
GLOSSARY

THE MOVIE GLOSSARY LEGEND

Charismatic Performer	CP	Invincible Optimist	IO
Chosen Adventurer	CA	Loyal Warrior	LW
Courageous Detective	CD	Magical Creator	MC
Dedicated Idealist	DI	Passionate Maverick	PM
Destined Hunter	DH	Rebellious Lover	RL
Determined Survivor	DS	Respected Champion	RC
Enlightened Healer	EH	Vivacious Romantic	VR
Existential Savior	ES	Youthful Sage	YS

1408 . . . . .ES
35 Up . . . . .DS
42 Up . . . . .DS
49 Up . . . . .DS
Abbott and Costello
  Meet Frankenstein . . . . .IO
Abbot and Costello
  Meet the Mummy . . . . .IO
About a Boy . . . . .YS, VR, EH
About Last Night . . . . .VR
About Schmidt . . . . .DS
Above the Rim . . . . .RC, LW
Absence of Malice . . . . .DI, CD, PM
Absent-Minded
  Professor, The . . . . .MC
Absolute Power . . . . .PM, CD
Abyss, The . . . . .CA
Accepted . . . . .YS, DI, RC
Accidental Tourist, The . . . . . .VR, DI, EH
Accused, The . . . . .DS, PM
Ace Ventura: Pet Detective . . .IO, RC
Aces High . . . . .LW, CA
Across the Universe . . . . .CP, VR
Adam's Rib . . . . .RC, VR
Adaptation . . . . .ES, CP
Addams Family, The . . . . . . .LW, ES
Addicted to Love . . . . .VR, RC
Adventures in Babysitting . . . .YS, LW
Adventures of Baron
  Munchausen, The . . . . .CA, MC
Adventures of Buckaroo

Banzai Across the 8th
  Dimension . . . . .CA
Adventures of Milo
  and Otis, The . . . . .CA, YS
Adventures of Priscilla,
  Queen of the Desert, The . . . .CP, MC
Adventures of Rin
  Tin Tin, The . . . . .CA, YS
Aeon Flux . . . . .ES, CA, PM
Affair to Remember, An . . . . .VR
African Queen, The . . . . .RL, PM
After Dark, My Sweet . . . . . . .PM, RL, DS
After Hours . . . . .ES, DI
Against All Odds . . . . .RL, RC
Age of Innocence, The . . . . . .RL, YS
Agnes of God . . . . .EH
Aguirre, the Wrath of God . . . .PM, CA
AI .YS, ES, MC
Air America . . . . .LW
Air Force One . . . . .PM, DH, LW
Air Up There, The . . . . .LW, RC
Airheads . . . . .CP, IO, DI
Airplane . . . . .IO
Airport 1975 . . . . .PM, DS
Akira . . . . .ES, YS, DH
Aladdin . . . . .MC, YS, CA
Alamo, The . . . . .PM, LW
Alex & Emma . . . . .VR
Alexander . . . . .PM, CA, LW
Alfie . . . . .VR, DI
Ali .RC, PM

Alice Doesn't Live
Here Anymore . . . . .DI, EH, CP
Alice in Wonderland . . . . .MC, YS, ES
Alien . . . . .DH
Alien Resurrection . . . . .DH, ES
Alien 3 . . . . .DH, ES
Aliens . . . . .DH
Aliens vs. Predator . . . . .DH
Alive . . . . .DS, LW
All About Eve . . . . .CP
All About My Mother . . . . .DS
All of Me . . . . .VR, EH, ES
All Quiet on the
Western Front . . . . .LW, DS
All That Heaven Allows . . . . . .RL, DS
All That Jazz . . . . .CP
All the King's Men . . . . .PM, DI
All the President's Men . . . . . .PM, CD, DI
All the Pretty Horses . . . . .RL, EH
All the Real Girls . . . . .RL, YS
All the Right Moves . . . . .RC, LW
Allan Quartermain
and the Lost City of Gold . . . .CA
Almost Famous . . . . .YS, CP, LW
Along Came a Spider . . . . .DH, CD
Along Came Polly . . . . .VR, IO
Alpha Dog . . . . .DH
Alphaville . . . . .CD
Altered States . . . . .ES, DH
Always . . . . .VR
Amadeus . . . . .CP
Amarcord . . . . .CP
Amazon Women
on the Moon . . . . .IO
Amélie . . . . .MC, VR
America's Sweethearts . . . . . . .VR, CP
American Anthem . . . . .RC
American Beauty . . . . .ES, DI
American Buffalo . . . . .PM
American Dreamz . . . . .CP, RC
American Gangster . . . . .PM
American Gigolo . . . . .PM, RL
American Graffiti . . . . .YS, LW
American Haunting, An . . . . . .DH
American History X . . . . .PM, EH
American in Paris, An . . . . . . .CP, VR
American Movie . . . . .DI
American Pie . . . . .YS, IO, LW
American President . . . . .PM, VR
American Psycho . . . . .DH
American Splendor . . . . .CP, DS, EH

American Tail, An . . . . .YS, CA
American Wedding . . . . .IO, VR
American Werewolf
in London, An . . . . .DH
Amistad . . . . .DS, PM
Amityville Horror, The . . . . . . .DH
Amores Perros . . . . .RL, PM
Amos & Andrew . . . . .LW
Anaconda . . . . .DH
Analyze This . . . . .IO, LW
Anastasia . . . . .YS, DS
Anatomy of a Murder . . . . . . .CD
Anchorman . . . . .IO, DI
And God Created Woman . . . .VR
And Justice for All . . . . .PM
Andrei Rublyov . . . . .CP, PM
Andromeda Strain, The . . . . . .ES
Angel Heart . . . . .ES, RL
Angela's Ashes . . . . .YS, DI, DS
Angels and Insects . . . . .VR
Angels in America . . . . .DS, MC
Angels in the Outfield . . . . . . .LW, MC
Angels with Dirty Faces . . . . . .PM
Anger Management . . . . .LW
Animal, The . . . . .IO
Animal Crackers . . . . .IO, DI
Animal House . . . . .RC, IO
Animatrix, The . . . . .ES
Anna Karenina . . . . .RL
Annie . . . . .CP, YS, DS
Annie Hall . . . . .VR, IO
Anniversary Party, The . . . . . . .DS, RL
Another 48 Hours . . . . .LW, IO
Ant Bully, The . . . . .YS, LW
Antwone Fisher . . . . .DS, EH
Antz .CA, LW
Any Given Sunday . . . . .LW, RC
Any Which Way You Can . . . .DI
Anything Else . . . . .IO, VR
Apartment, The . . . . .VR, DI
Apocalypse Now . . . . .DH
Apocalypto . . . . .DH

Charismatic Performer: CP • Chosen Adventurer: CA •
Courageous Detective: CD • Dedicated Idealist: DI •
Destined Hunter: DH • Determined Survivor: DS •
Enlightened Healer: EH • Existential Savior: ES •
Invincible Optimist: IO • Loyal Warrior: LW •
Magical Creator: MC • Passionate Maverick: PM •
Rebellious Lover: RL • Respected Champion: RC •
Vivacious Romantic: VR • Youthful Sage: YS

Beaches . . . . .DS, EH, LW
Bear, The . . . . .DH
Beastmaster, The . . . . .DH, CA
Beautiful Girls . . . . .VR, LW
Beautiful Mind, A . . . . .MC, EH
Beauty and the Beast . . . . . . .RL, MC
Beavis and Butthead
   Do America . . . . .YS, IO, CA
Because of Winn Dixie . . . . . .YS, LW
Becket . . . . .RL, PM
Bed of Roses . . . . .VR
Bedazzled . . . . .MC, VR, IO
Bedknobs and Broomsticks . . .MC
Bedtime for Bonzo . . . . .LW, DI
Bee Movie . . . . .DI, VR
Beerfest . . . . .IO, RC
Beethoven . . . . .YS, RC
Beetlejuice . . . . .MC
Before Night Falls . . . . .DS, PM, MC
Before Sunrise . . . . .VR
Before Sunset . . . . .RL
Behind Enemy Lines . . . . .CA
Being John Malkovich . . . . . .ES
Being Julia . . . . .CP, DS, RL
Being There . . . . .PM, EH, MC
Bellboy, The . . . . .IO
Belle du Jour . . . . .CP, RL
Bells of St. Mary's, The . . . . . .EH
Beloved . . . . .DS
Bend It Like Beckham . . . . . . .RC, LW
Ben-Hur . . . . .CA
Benny and Joon . . . . .VR, CP
Beowulf . . . . .CA, DH
Best in Show . . . . .IO, RC
Best Laid Plans . . . . .RL, DI
Best Man, The . . . . .VR, LW
Best of Times, The . . . . .LW, DI
Best Years of Our Lives, The . . .DS, LW
Better Off Dead . . . . .RC, IO
Better Tomorrow, A . . . . .DH, CD
Betty Blue . . . . .DI, DS, RL
Beverly Hills Cop . . . . .IO, CD
Bewitched . . . . .MC, VR
Beyond, The . . . . .DH
Beyond the Valley
   of the Dolls . . . . .CP, VR
Bicycle Thief, The . . . . .YS, DS
Big . . . . .YS, DI
Big Blue, The . . . . .CA
Big Bounce, The . . . . .IO, DI
Big Chill, The . . . . .VR, DS, LW

Big Daddy . . . . .IO, LW
Big Easy, The . . . . .CD
Big Fish . . . . .MC
Big Jake . . . . .DH, PM
Big Lebowski, The . . . . .ES, DI, LW
Big Momma's House . . . . .CP, IO
Big Night . . . . .DI
Big Picture, The . . . . .CP, IO
Big Red One, The . . . . .LW
Big Sleep, The . . . . .CD
Big Trouble . . . . .DI, RC
Big Trouble in Little China . . . .DH
Bill & Ted's Bogus Journey . . . .IO, YS
Bill & Ted's Excellent
   Adventure . . . . .IO, YS
Billy Bathgate . . . . .PM
Billy Elliot . . . . .YS, CP
Billy Jack . . . . .PM, LW
Billy Madison . . . . .RC, IO
Biloxi Blues . . . . .YS, LW
Bio-Dome . . . . .IO
Bird on a Wire . . . . .CA, VR
Bird .CP
Birdcage, The . . . . .CP, IO, VR
Birdman of Alcatraz . . . . .PM, DS, LW
Birds, The . . . . .DS, DH, CD
Birth .ES, YS, RL
Birth of a Nation, The . . . . . . .DS, PM
Black Book . . . . .PM
Black Dahlia, The . . . . .CD
Black Hawk Down . . . . .LW, DH
Black Hole, The . . . . .ES, CA
Black Orpheus . . . . .CP, VR
Black Rain . . . . .CD, PM
Black Snake Moan . . . . .DS, RL, DI
Black Stallion, The . . . . .YS, DS, RC
Black Sunday . . . . .DH
Black Widow . . . . .DH, RL
Blackboard Jungle . . . . .YS, PM
Blacula . . . . .DH
Bladerunner . . . . .DH, CD
Blades of Glory . . . . .IO, RC

Charismatic Performer: CP • Chosen Adventurer: CA •
Courageous Detective: CD • Dedicated Idealist: DI •
Destined Hunter: DH • Determined Survivor: DS •
Enlightened Healer: EH • Existential Savior: ES •
Invincible Optimist: IO • Loyal Warrior: LW •
Magical Creator: MC • Passionate Maverick: PM •
Rebellious Lover: RL • Respected Champion: RC •
Vivacious Romantic: VR • Youthful Sage: YS

Planet, The . . . . .ES, CA	Captain Blood . . . . .PM, CA
Brother . . . . .PM, DI, LW	Captain Corelli's Mandolin . . . .RL, CP, PM
Brother's Keeper . . . . .CD, DS	Captain Ron . . . . .IO, LW
Brotherhood of the Wolf . . . . .DH	Capturing the Friedmans . . . . .DS
Brothers Grimm, The . . . . . . .CA, ES	Car Wash . . . . .DI
Brothers McMullen . . . . .VR, LW	Career Girls . . . . .DI
Brown Bunny, The . . . . .CP	Career Opportunities . . . . .DI
Bruce Almighty . . . . .MC, VR	Carla's Song . . . . .DS, CD
Bubba Ho Tep . . . . .ES, DH	Carlito's Way . . . . .PM, DI
Bubble Boy . . . . .IO	Carmen Jones . . . . .PM
Buddy Holly Story, The . . . . . .CP	Carnal Knowledge . . . . .RL
Buffalo '66 . . . . .VR, EH	Carnival of Souls . . . . .DH
Bug .DH	Carousel . . . . .RL, CP
Bug's Life, A . . . . .VR, YS	Carrie . . . . .DH
Bugsy Malone . . . . .YS	Cars . . . . .YS, CA
Bugsy . . . . .PM, DI	Casa de los Babys . . . . .DS, LW, EH
Bull Durham . . . . .RC, VR	Casablanca . . . . .RL, PM
Bulletproof Monk . . . . .DH	Casanova . . . . .VR
Bullets Over Broadway . . . . . .CP	Casino Royale . . . . .PM, CA
Bullitt . . . . .PM	Casino . . . . .PM, LW
Bully . . . . .DS, YS	Casper . . . . .YS, MC
Bulworth . . . . .PM, CP	Cast Away . . . . .DS, DI
Burbs, The . . . . .IO, CD	Castle of Cagliostro . . . . .CA
Bus Stop . . . . .VR, CP	Cat Ballou . . . . .VR, PM
Business of Strangers, The . . . .DS	Cat in the Hat . . . . .MC, YS
Bustin' Loose . . . . .IO, DI	Cat on a Hot Tin Roof . . . . . . .DS
But I'm a Cheerleader . . . . . . .DS, YS	Cat People . . . . .DH, RL
Butch Cassidy and the	Cat Returns, The . . . . .MC, YS
Sundance Kid . . . . .LW, PM	Cat's Eye . . . . .DH
Butcher's Wife, The . . . . .VR, MC	Cat's Meow, The . . . . .DS, RL
Butterflies are Free . . . . .DS, VR, EH	Catch a Fire . . . . .PM
Butterfly Effect, The . . . . .ES	Catch Me If You Can . . . . .CP, PM, DI
Bye Bye Birdie . . . . .CP, YS, VR	Catch-22 . . . . .ES
	Cats and Dogs . . . . .RC
Cabaret . . . . .CP, RL	Catwoman . . . . .PM, MC
Cabinet of Dr. Caligari . . . . . . .ES, DH	Caveman . . . . .IO
Cable Guy, The . . . . .DH, IO	Cecil B. Demented . . . . .CP, PM
Caddyshack . . . . .RC	Celebration, The . . . . .VR
Caine Mutiny . . . . .PM, LW	Celebrity . . . . .CP
Calendar Girl . . . . .YS, LW	Cell, The . . . . .CD, ES
California Split . . . . .DS, LW, DI	Center Stage . . . . .CP, RC
California Suite . . . . .VR, DI	Central Station . . . . .DS, LW
Camelot . . . . .VR, CA	
Cameraman, The . . . . .PM	
Can't Buy Me Love . . . . .VR	
Can't Hardly Wait . . . . .YS, RC	
Candidate, The . . . . .PM	
Candyman . . . . .DH	
Cannonball Run . . . . .RC, IO	
Cape Fear . . . . .DH	
Capote . . . . .EH, CP	

Charismatic Performer: CP • Chosen Adventurer: CA •
Courageous Detective: CD • Dedicated Idealist: DI •
Destined Hunter: DH • Determined Survivor: DS •
Enlightened Healer: EH • Existential Savior: ES •
Invincible Optimist: IO • Loyal Warrior: LW •
Magical Creator: MC • Passionate Maverick: PM •
Rebellious Lover: RL • Respected Champion: RC •
Vivacious Romantic: VR • Youthful Sage: YS

Conformist, The . . . . .DH
Congo . . . . .DH, CA
Connecticut Yankee, A . . . . . . .CA, DI, MC
Connie and Carla . . . . .CP
Conspiracy Theory . . . . .CA
Constant Gardener, The . . . . . .PM, DS
Constantine . . . . .DH, ES
Contact . . . . .PM, ES
Contempt . . . . .RL
Contender, The . . . . .PM
Conversation, The . . . . .CD, PM
Cook, the Thief, His Wife
  and Her Lover, The . . . . . . .RL, DI
Cookie's Fortune . . . . .CP
Cool Hand Luke . . . . .PM
Cool Runnings . . . . .RC, LW
Cool World . . . . .ES
Cooler, The . . . . .EH
Cop Land . . . . .PM, LW
Copycat . . . . .DH
Coraline . . . . .YS, CA, MC
Corky Romano . . . . .IO
Corpse Bride . . . . .RL, MC, ES
Corrina Corrina . . . . .EH, YS
Cotton Club, The . . . . .CP
Count of Monte
  Cristo, The . . . . .CP, PM, DH
Courage Under Fire . . . . .PM, LW
Court Jester . . . . .CP, IO
Cousin, Cousine . . . . .RL
Cousins . . . . .RL
Covenant, The . . . . .DH
Cowboy Bebop . . . . .CA, ES
Cowboys, The . . . . .LW
Coyote Ugly . . . . .DI, CP, VR
CQ .PM, CP
Cradle Will Rock . . . . .DI, CP
Crank . . . . .DH
Crash . . . . .DS
Crazy/Beautiful . . . . .RL, YS
Creature from the Black
  Lagoon, The . . . . .DH
Creepshow . . . . .DH, ES
Crimes and Misdemeanors . . . .VR, ES
Crimes of the Heart . . . . .DS
Crimson Tide . . . . .CA, PM
Critical Care . . . . .EH, DI
Crocodile Dundee . . . . .IO, VR
Cromwell . . . . .PM
Crooklyn . . . . .DI
Crossing Delancey . . . . .VR

Crossing Guard . . . . .DS
Crossover . . . . .LW
Crouching Tiger,
  Hidden Dragon . . . . .RL, MC, CA, EH
Croupier . . . . .DI, CD
Crow, The . . . . .DH, ES
Crucible, The . . . . .DS
Cruel Intentions . . . . .RL, RC
Crumb . . . . .CP, ES
Cry-Baby . . . . .CP, YS
Cry Freedom . . . . .DS, PM
Crying Game, The . . . . .RL, DS, CP, EH
Cube . . . . .DH, ES
Cujo . . . . .DH
Curdled . . . . .DH
Curious George . . . . .CA, YS
Curly Sue . . . . .YS, EH
Curse of the Jade
  Scorpion, The . . . . .CD, IO, VR
Cutthroat Island . . . . .CA
Cutting Edge, The . . . . .RC, VR
Cyrano de Bergerac . . . . .CP, VR

D.O.A. . . . . .CD
Da Vinci Code, The . . . . .CD, CA
Dad . . . . .LW, EH
Daddy Day Care . . . . .DI, IO
Dahmer . . . . .DH
Dallas . . . . .PM, DI
Dance with Me . . . . .CP, RC
Dancer in the Dark . . . . .DI, ES, CP, DS
Dances with Wolves . . . . .CA, RL
Dangerous Beauty . . . . .RL
Dangerous Liasons . . . . .CP, RL, RC
Dangerous Minds . . . . .EH, YS
Daredevil . . . . .CA
Dark City . . . . .ES,
Dark City . . . . .ES, DH
Dark Crystal, The . . . . .MC, YS, CA
Dark Half, The . . . . .DH, ES
Dark Knight, The . . . . .CA
Darkman . . . . .DH

Dogtown and Z-Boys	RC, PM
Dogville	DS
Dolores Claiborne	DS, EH,CD
Dominick and Eugene	DS, LW
Domino	DH, PM
Don Juan DeMarco	VR, CP
Don't Look Back	CP, PM
Don't Look Now	ES, DH
Don't Say a Word	CD, DH
Don't Tell Mom the Babysitter's Dead	DI, YS
Donnie Brasco	PM
Donnie Darko	ES, YS
Doom	DH
Door in the Floor, The	DS
Doors, The	CP
Double Indemnity	CD
Double Jeopardy	DS, DH
Down and Out in Beverly Hills	DI, YS, LW
Down by Law	ES
Down with Love	CP, VR
Downfall	PM
Dr. Jekyll and Mr. Hyde	DH, MC, ES
Dr. No	CA, PM
Dr. Strangelove	ES, PM
Dr. Zhivago	RL, DS, PM
Dracula	DH, RL
Dragnet	DI, IO
Dragonheart	LW, CA
Dream a Little Dream	ES, YS
Dreamer, The	YS
Dreamers, The	RL, YS
Dreamgirls	CP
Dreams	ES
Dreamscape	ES
Dressed to Kill	DH, CD
Driving Miss Daisy	EH, LW
Drop Dead Fred	MC
Drop Dead Gorgeous	CP, RC
Drugstore Cowboy	PM, ES
Drumline	CP, LW, RC
Drunken Master	DH
Duck Season	YS, LW
Duck Soup	IO, CP
Dude, Where's My Car?	IO, ES
Duel	DH
Duel in the Sun	DS, RL
Duellists, The	RC, DS
Duets	CP, VR
Dukes of Hazzard, The	IO, RC

Dumb and Dumber	IO
Dumbo	YS, RC
Dune	PM, CA, DH
Dungeons and Dragons	CA, YS, MC
Duplex	DI, VR
E.T.	YS, CA, EH
Earth Girls Are Easy	IO
Earth vs. the Flying Saucers	DH, ES
Earthquake	DS
East of Eden	PM
Easy Money	IO, RC
Easy Rider	PM, LW
Eat Drink Man Woman	VR
Eating Raoul	ES
Ed Gein	DH
Ed Wood	CP, PM, MC
Edge, The	DH
Edmond	PM, ES
Educating Rita	EH, VR
Edward Scissorhands	MC, RL
8 1/2	CP, ES
8 Femmes	CP, CD, ES
Eight Men Out	RC, LW
8 Mile	CP, DS, PM
88 Minutes	DH
84 Charing Cross Road	DI, VR
El Cid	CA, PM
El Dorado	PM, DH
El Mariachi	DH
Election	RC, YS, DI
Elektra	CA
Elephant	YS, DS
Elephant Man, The	EH
Elevator to the Gallows	CD, DH
Elf	MC, IO
Elizabeth	RL, PM
Elizabethtown	VR, DS, DI
Ella Enchanted	MC, YS, RC
Emma	VR
Emperor's New Groove, The	YS, RC
Empire of the Sun	YS, DS, CA

Charismatic Performer: CP • Chosen Adventurer: CA •
Courageous Detective: CD • Dedicated Idealist: DI •
Destined Hunter: DH • Determined Survivor: DS •
Enlightened Healer: EH • Existential Savior: ES •
Invincible Optimist: IO • Loyal Warrior: LW •
Magical Creator: MC • Passionate Maverick: PM •
Rebellious Lover: RL • Respected Champion: RC •
Vivacious Romantic: VR • Youthful Sage: YS

Feeling Minnesota . . . . .VR
Fellini-Satyricon . . . . .YS, ES, DS
Femme Fatale . . . . .DH, CD
Ferris Bueller's Day Off . . . . . . .YS, RC
Fever Pitch . . . . .VR, RC
Few Good Men, A . . . . .PM, CD, LW
Fiddler on the Roof . . . . .LW, CP, DI
Field of Dreams . . . . .MC, RC
Fifth Element, The . . . . .ES, CA, DH
50 First Dates . . . . .VR, EH
Fight Club . . . . .ES, LW, PM
Final Cut, The . . . . .ES, DI
Final Destination . . . . .DH
Final Fantasy . . . . .ES, CA
Find Me Guilty . . . . .PM
Finding Forrester . . . . .LW, YS
Finding Nemo . . . . .YS, CA
Finding Neverland . . . . .MC, YS, EH
Fine Mess, A . . . . .DI
Fire and Ice . . . . .MC, CA
Fire in the Sky . . . . .ES
Firestarter . . . . .YS, DH
Firewall . . . . .DH
Firm, The . . . . .PM, DI
First Blood . . . . .DH
First Knight . . . . .VR, CA, LW
First Wives Club, The . . . . . . .PM, LW, VR
Fish Called Wanda, A . . . . . . .DI, LW
Fisher King, The . . . . .MC, ES, EH
Fistful of Dollars, A . . . . .DH, PM
Five Easy Pieces . . . . .PM
Flags of Our Fathers . . . . .LW
Flash Gordon . . . . .CA
Flashdance . . . . .CP, VR
Flatliners . . . . .ES, EH
Flawless . . . . .LW, CP
Flesh . . . . .ES
Flesh and Bone . . . . .RL
Fletch . . . . .IO, DI
Fletch Lives . . . . .IO, DI
Flight of the Navigator . . . . . . .YS, CA, ES
Flightplan . . . . .ES, CD
Flintstones, The . . . . .LW, DI
Flipper . . . . .YS, LW
Flirt .VR
Flirting with Disaster . . . . .IO, LW
Flubber . . . . .MC, YS
Flushed Away . . . . .YS, CA
Fly, The . . . . .ES, DH, RL
Fly Away Home . . . . .YS, CA
Flyboys . . . . .LW

Fog, The . . . . .DH
Fools Rush In . . . . .VR, DI
Footloose . . . . .CP, VR, RC, YS
For a Few Dollars More . . . . . .DH, PM
For Keeps . . . . .YS, VR
For the Boys . . . . .CP, VR
40 Year Old Virgin . . . . .IO, VR, DI
48 Hours . . . . .LW, IO
49 Up . . . . .DI, ES
42nd Street . . . . .CP, RC
For Whom the Bell Tolls . . . . .PM, RL
For Your Consideration . . . . . . .IO, CP
For Your Eyes Only . . . . .PM, CA
Forbidden Planet . . . . .CA
Forces of Nature . . . . .VR
Forget Paris . . . . .VR
Forrest Gump . . . . .MC, CA
Fortress . . . . .DH, ES
Fortune Cookie, The . . . . .MC, VR
Foul Play . . . . .VR
Fountain, The . . . . .CA, ES, EH
Four Brothers . . . . .PM, LW
Four Feathers, The . . . . .CA, VR, LW
Four Little Girls . . . . .DS
Four Rooms . . . . .DI, IO, ES
400 Blows . . . . .YS, ES
Four Weddings and
   a Funeral . . . . .VR, IO
1492 . . . . .PM, CA
Fox and the Hound, The . . . . .YS, VR
Frailty . . . . .DH, ES, YS
Frankenstein . . . . .MC
Frankenweenie . . . . .MC, YS
Frankie and Johnny . . . . .VR
Frantic . . . . .ES
Freaks . . . . .DH
Freaky Friday . . . . .YS, IO, RC
Freddy Got Fingered . . . . .IO
Free Willy . . . . .YS, LW
Freedom Writers . . . . .EH, PM, EH, YS
Freeway . . . . .DH
French Connection, The . . . . . .CD, PM

French Kiss .... VR, CP
Frenzy .... DH
Frequency .... ES, LW
Fresh .... YS, DS
Freshman, The .... LW
Frida .... CP, VR, DS, EH
Friday .... IO
Friday Night Lights .... LW, RC, YS
Friday the 13th .... DH
Fried Green Tomatoes ...... DS, RL
Friends with Money .... RL, DI
Fright Night .... DH
Frighteners, The .... DH, ES
Frisco Kid, The .... LW
Fritz the Cat .... ES
From Dusk Till Dawn .... DH
From Hell .... CD, DH
From Here to Eternity ...... RL, LW
From Justin to Kelly .... CP, VR
From Russia with Love ..... CA, PM
Fugitive, The .... CA
Full Frontal .... CP
Full Metal Jacket .... DH
Full Monty, The .... DI, CP
Fun with Dick and Jane ..... DI, VR
Funny Farm .... DI, YS
Funny Girl .... CP, VR
Funny Thing Happened on
  the Way to the Forum, A ... IO, VR, MC

Gacy .... DH
Galaxy Quest .... IO, CA
Game, The .... CD, ES
Gandhi .... PM, EH
Gangs of New York .... PM, DH
Garbage Pail Kids Movie ..... YS
Garden State .... DS, VR, YS, EH
Garfield .... IO
Gas, Food Lodging .... MC, RL, DS
Gaslight .... DS
Gate, The .... DH
Gattaca .... ES
Gay Divorcee, The .... CP, VR
General, The .... CA
Gentlemen Prefer Blondes ... CP, IO
Gentlemen's Agreement ..... PM, DS
George of the Jungle .... CA, IO
Get Carter .... DH
Get on the Bus .... LW
Get Rich or Die Tryin' ...... DI, PM, CP
Get Shorty .... PM, RC

Get Smart .... IO, CD
Getaway, The .... PM, RL
Ghost .... VR, CD
Ghost and Mr. Chicken, The .. IO
Ghost and Mrs. Muir, The .... RL, EH
Ghost and the Darkness, The .. DH, LW
Ghost Bride .... RL, MC
Ghost Dog .... DH
Ghost in the Machine .... DH, ES
Ghost in the Shell .... ES, DH
Ghost Rider .... PM, DH
Ghost World .... YS, RL, EH
Ghostbusters .... IO, CA
Ghostbusters 2 .... IO, CA
Ghosts of Mars .... DH
G.I. Jane .... PM
Gia .... DS
Gift, The .... ES, DH
Gigi .... VR, YS, CP
Gigli .... VR
Gilda .... CP, RL, CD
Gimme Shelter .... CP
Ginger Snaps .... DH
Girl 6 .... RL, DI
Girl Can't Help It, The .... VR
Girl Crazy .... CP, VR
Girl Interrupted .... DS
Girl Next Door, The .... YS, DI
Girlfight .... PM
Girls Just Wanna Have Fun .. IO, RC
Gladiator .... PM, CA, DH, RC
Glass Shield, The .... DS, PM
Glengarry Glen Ross .... DI
Glitter .... CP
Gloria .... DS, YS
Glory .... LW, PM
Go .... CA, ES
Godfather, The .... LW, PM
Godfather: Part II, The ...... PM, LW
Godfather: Part III, The ..... PM, LW, RL
Gods and Generals .... LW, PM
Gods Must Be Crazy, The .... IO
Godzilla .... DH
Going My Way .... EH
Gold Rush, The .... PM
Golden Child, The .... CA, IO, MC
Golden Compass, The ...... CA, YS, MC
Goldeneye .... PM, CA
Goldfinger .... CA, PM
Gone in 60 seconds .... PM
Gone with the Wind .... DS, RL, DI

Good Boy . . . . .YS, LW
Good German, The . . . . .CD
Good Girl, The . . . . .EH, RL, DI
Good Morning, Vietnam . . . . .CP, LW
Good Night and Good Luck . . .PM
Good Shepherd, The . . . . . . .PM, LW
Good Son, The . . . . .YS, DH
Good Will Hunting . . . . .EH, DI
Good, the Bad, and
  the Ugly, The . . . . .DH, PM
Goodbye Columbus . . . . .VR
Goodbye Girl, The . . . . .VR, CP
Goodfellas . . . . .PM, LW, DI
Goodbye, Mr. Chips . . . . .EH, LW
Goonies, The . . . . .CA, YS, LW
Gorillas in the Mist . . . . .PM, EH
Gosford Park . . . . .CD, DI
Gothic . . . . .ES
Gothika . . . . .DH, ES
Graduate, The . . . . .RL, VR, YS
Grand Canyon . . . . .EH, ES
Grand Hotel . . . . .VR
Grand Illusion . . . . .LW, DS
Grand Theft Parsons . . . . . . .DI
Grapes of Wrath, The . . . . . .DI, LW
Grave of the Fireflies . . . . . . .DS, ES
Graveyard Shift . . . . .DH
Gray's Anatomy . . . . .DI, PM
Grease . . . . .VR, IO, LW
Great Balls of Fire . . . . .CP, RL
Great Dictator, The . . . . .PM, IO
Great Escape, The . . . . .PM, LW
Great Expectations . . . . .YS, RL
Great Gatsby, The . . . . .MC, DI
Great Muppet Caper, The . . . . .CA, YS, MC
Great Outdoors, The . . . . . . .RC, IO
Great Race, The . . . . .RC, MC
Great Waldo Pepper, The . . . . .MC
Great Ziegfeld, The . . . . .PM
Greatest Show on
  Earth, The . . . . .CP, MC
Greatest Story Ever
  Told, The . . . . .EH
Green Card . . . . .VR
Green Mile, The . . . . .EH, IO
Green Street Hooligans . . . . . .DS, RC, LW
Gremlins . . . . .DH
Grey Gardens . . . . .DS
Greystroke . . . . .PM, EH, RL
Gridiron Gang . . . . .LW, RC
Grifters, The . . . . .PM, DI

Grim, The . . . . .DH, CA, RL
Grinch, The . . . . .MC, YS
Grindhouse . . . . .DH
Grizzly Man . . . . .PM
Gross Anatomy . . . . .VR, DI
Grosse Point Blank . . . . .VR, IO, DI
Groundhog Day . . . . .VR, IO, ES
Grudge, The . . . . .DH
Grumpy Old Men . . . . .LW
Guerrilla . . . . .PM
Guess Who's Coming
  to Dinner . . . . .RL
Gun Shy . . . . .CD, EH
Gung Ho . . . . .DI
Gunga Din . . . . .PM
Guns of Navarone, The . . . . . .LW, PM
Guys and Dolls . . . . .CP, VR
Gypsy . . . . .CP

Hackers . . . . .YS, PM
Haiku Tunnel . . . . .DI
Hail the Conquering Hero . . . .DS, LW, CP
Hairspray . . . . .CP, YS
Half Baked . . . . .IO, DI
Half Nelson . . . . .EH, YS, DS
Halloween . . . . .DH
Halo . . . . .DH, CA
Hamburger Hill . . . . .LW, DH
Hamlet . . . . .ES, DH
Hands on a Hard Body . . . . . .IO, DI, RC
Hang 'Em High . . . . .DH, PM
Hanky Panky . . . . .VR, IO
Hannah and Her Sisters . . . . . .VR, LW
Hannibal . . . . .CD, DH
Happily N'Ever After . . . . .MC
Happiness . . . . .DS, ES
Happy Feet . . . . .CP, PM, RC
Happy Feet . . . . .CP, VR, YS
Happy Gilmore . . . . .RC, IO
Hard Boiled . . . . .DH, PM
Hard Day's Night, A . . . . .CP, IO
Hard Eight . . . . .EH

Charismatic Performer: CP • Chosen Adventurer: CA •
Courageous Detective: CD • Dedicated Idealist: DI •
Destined Hunter: DH • Determined Survivor: DS •
Enlightened Healer: EH • Existential Savior: ES •
Invincible Optimist: IO • Loyal Warrior: LW •
Magical Creator: MC • Passionate Maverick: PM •
Rebellious Lover: RL • Respected Champion: RC •
Vivacious Romantic: VR • Youthful Sage: YS

Charismatic Performer: CP • Chosen Adventurer: CA •
Courageous Detective: CD • Dedicated Idealist: DI •
Destined Hunter: DH • Determined Survivor: DS •
Enlightened Healer: EH • Existential Savior: ES •
Invincible Optimist: IO • Loyal Warrior: LW •
Magical Creator: MC • Passionate Maverick: PM •
Rebellious Lover: RL • Respected Champion: RC •
Vivacious Romantic: VR • Youthful Sage: YS

Lord of Illusions . . . . .DH, ES
Lord of the Flies . . . . .DH, YS, LW
Lord of the Rings:
  Fellowship of the Rings . . . . .CA, MC, DH
Lord of the Rings:
  The Return of the King . . . . .CA, MC, DH
Lord of the Rings:
  The Two Towers . . . . .CA, MC, DH
Lord of War . . . . .PM
Lords of Dogtown . . . . .YS, PM, RC
Lorenzo's Oil . . . . .EH
Losing Isaiah . . . . .DS
Lost Boys, The . . . . .YS, DH, ES
Lost Highway . . . . .ES, CD
Lost in Translation . . . . .RL
Lost in Yonkers . . . . .LW, YS, VR
Lost Skeleton of
  Cadavra, The . . . . .IO
Lost Weekend, The . . . . .DS
Lost World, The . . . . .DH, CA
Lot Like Love, A . . . . .VR
Love Actually . . . . .VR
Love Affair . . . . .VR, DI
Love and Death . . . . .VR, IO
Love Bug, The . . . . .YS, MC,
Love in the Afternoon . . . . . . .VR
Love Is a Many Spendored Thing   RL
Love Is the Devil . . . . .CP, RL, DS
Love Jones . . . . .VR
Love Me If You Dare . . . . .RL
Love Me Tender . . . . .VR
Love Story . . . . .VR, RL
Love with a Proper Stranger . . .VR
Lovely and Amazing . . . . .EH
Loverboy . . . . .DI, VR
Lucas .YS, RC, LW

M . . . . .DH
M. Butterfly . . . . .RL, CP
Ma Vie En Rose . . . . .YS, MC, CP
Macbeth . . . . .PM, DH
Machinist, The . . . . .ES
Mad Dog and Glory . . . . .CP, IO, VR
Mad Max . . . . .DH, PM
Madagascar . . . . .CA
Made .LW
Made in America . . . . .IO, LW
Made in Heaven . . . . .RL
Madness of King George,
  The .PM, MC
Magnificent Ambersons,

The .DI, VR
Magnificent Obsession . . . . . .RL
Magnificent Seven, The . . . . . .DH, LW, PM
Magnolia . . . . .DS, ES
Magnum Force . . . . .DH, PM
Maid in Manhattan . . . . .VR, DI
Major League . . . . .RC, IO
Making Mr. Right . . . . .MC, VR
Malcolm X . . . . .PM
Malena . . . . .RL, DS, YS
Mallrats . . . . .IO, VR, RC
Maltese Falcon, The . . . . .CD
Man and a Woman, A . . . . . . .VR
Man Bites Dog . . . . .DH
Man for All Seasons, A . . . . . .PM, RL
Man for All Seasons, A . . . . . .RL, PM
Man from Elysian
  Fields, The . . . . .CP
Man from Snowy River, The . . . .PM
Man in the Iron Mask, The . . .PM, LW
Man in the Moon, The . . . . . . .YS, DS
Man of the Year . . . . .PM, DI, CP
Man of La Mancha . . . . .PM, CP, DI
Man on Fire . . . . .DH, YS
Man on the Moon . . . . .CP, ES
Man Who Came to
  Dinner, The . . . . .IO
Man Who Fell to
  Earth, The . . . . .ES, MC
Man Who Knew Too
  Much, The . . . . .CD
Man Who Shot Liberty
  Valence, The . . . . .DH
Man Who Wasn't There,
  The .ES, DI
Man Who Would be King,
  The .CA
Man with One Red Shoe,
  The .IO
Man with the Golden Arm,
  The .DS, EH
Man with the Golden Gun,
  The .PM, CA

Charismatic Performer: CP • Chosen Adventurer: CA •
Courageous Detective: CD • Dedicated Idealist: DI •
Destined Hunter: DH • Determined Survivor: DS •
Enlightened Healer: EH • Existential Savior: ES •
Invincible Optimist: IO • Loyal Warrior: LW •
Magical Creator: MC • Passionate Maverick: PM •
Rebellious Lover: RL • Respected Champion: RC •
Vivacious Romantic: VR • Youthful Sage: YS

Miracle on 34th Street . . . . . . .MC
Miracle Worker, The . . . . .EH, YS
Mirror Has Two Faces, The . . . .VR
MirrorMask . . . . .YS, MC, ES, CA
Misery . . . . .DH
Miss Congeniality . . . . .CP, VR, RC
Miss Potter . . . . .MC, VR
Mission, The . . . . .PM
Mission: Impossible . . . . .CA
Mississippi Burning . . . . .DS, PM, CD
Mississippi Masala . . . . .RL, LW
Mister Roberts . . . . .DI
Mo Better Blues . . . . .CP
Moby Dick . . . . .CA
Modern Problems . . . . .VR, DI
Modern Romance . . . . .VR, DI, IO
Modern Times . . . . .IO, PM
Moll Flanders . . . . .DS, EH
Mommie Dearest . . . . .DS
Mona Lisa Smile . . . . .EH, LW
Money Pit, The . . . . .DI, VR
Money Talks . . . . .IO, LW, DI, RC
Monkey Business . . . . .MC
Monkeybone . . . . .ES, CP, IO
Monsoon Wedding . . . . .RL
Monster . . . . .PM, DH, RL
Monster House . . . . .YS, CA
Monster's Ball . . . . .DS
Monster's Ball . . . . .DS, EH
Monsters, Inc. . . . . .MC, YS, DI
Monty Python and the
   Holy Grail . . . . .IO
Monty Python's Life
   of Brian . . . . .IO
Monty Python's The
   Meaning of Life . . . . .IO, ES
Moolaadé . . . . .EH, PM
Moon Over Parador . . . . .CP, IO
Moonlight Mile . . . . .RL, DS, EH
Moonraker . . . . .PM, CA
Moonstruck . . . . .VR, DI
Morning After, The . . . . .ES, CD
Mortal Thoughts . . . . .DS, CD
Morvern Callar . . . . .DS, CP
Mosquito Coast, The . . . . . . .PM, ES
Mothman Prophecies, The . . . .ES
Motorcycle Diaries, The . . . . .PM, LW
Moulin Rouge . . . . .RL, CP
Mouse Hunt . . . . .IO
Mouse That Roared, The . . . .IO, PM
Moving Violations . . . . .IO, RC

Mr. and Mrs. Smith . . . . .VR, DH
Mr. Blandings Builds His
   Dream House . . . . .DI
Mr. Deeds . . . . .IO, DI
Mr. Deeds Goes to Town . . . . .IO, DI
Mr. Holland's Opus . . . . .CP, LW
Mr. Magorium's Wonder
   Emporium . . . . .YS, MC
Mr. Mom . . . . .DI, LW
Mr. Skeffington . . . . .DS, VR, CP
Mr. Smith Goes to
   Washington . . . . .DI, PM
Mrs. Brown . . . . .EH
Mrs. Doubtfire . . . . .CP, MC, YS
Mrs. Henderson Presents . . . . .CP, PM
Mrs. Miniver . . . . .DS
Mrs. Parker and the Vicious
   Circle . . . . .CP, RL
Much Ado About Nothing . . . .VR, RC
Mulholland Drive . . . . .ES
Mulan . . . . .CA, YS
Mulholland Falls . . . . .CD
Multiplicity . . . . .DI, VR
Mummy, The . . . . .CA
Munich . . . . .DH, LW, PM
Muppet Movie, The . . . . .MC, CP
Muppets from Space . . . . . . .MC, CP
Muppets Take Manhattan,
   The . . . . .MC, CP
Murder at 1600 . . . . .CD
Murder by Death . . . . .CD, IO
Murder in the First . . . . .DS, PM, LW
Murder on the Orient Express . .CD
Murderball . . . . .DS, RC
Muriel's Wedding . . . . .VR, RC
Murphy's Romance . . . . .VR
Muse, The . . . . .CP, VR
Music and Lyrics . . . . .VR, CP
Music Box, The . . . . .DS
Music Man, The . . . . .DI, VR, CP
Music of the Heart . . . . .CP, LW
Musketeer, The . . . . .CA

Charismatic Performer: CP ∘ Chosen Adventurer: CA ∘
Courageous Detective: CD ∘ Dedicated Idealist: DI ∘
Destined Hunter: DH ∘ Determined Survivor: DS ∘
Enlightened Healer: EH ∘ Existential Savior: ES ∘
Invincible Optimist: IO ∘ Loyal Warrior: LW ∘
Magical Creator: MC ∘ Passionate Maverick: PM ∘
Rebellious Lover: RL ∘ Respected Champion: RC ∘
Vivacious Romantic: VR ∘ Youthful Sage: YS

Nixon . . . . .PM
No Escape . . . . .DH
No Holds Barred . . . . .RC
No Reservations . . . . .VR
No Way Out . . . . .CD, RL
Nobody's Fool . . . . .VR
Noises Off . . . . .CP, IO
Norma Rae . . . . .PM, DI
North by Northwest . . . . .DH, CD
North Country . . . . .DI, PM
North Dallas Forty . . . . .RC, LW
North Shore . . . . .RC, LW
Nosferatu . . . . .DH
Not of This Earth . . . . .ES, IO
Not Without My Daughter . . .DS
Notebook, The . . . . .VR, EH
Nothing in Common . . . . .LW, EH
Notorious . . . . .RL, CD
Notting Hill . . . . .VR, CP
Now and Then . . . . .YS, LW, EH, DS
Now, Voyager . . . . .RL, DS
Number 23, The . . . . .ES
Nun's Story, The . . . . .EH
Nurse Betty . . . . .EH
Nutty Professor, The . . . . .MC, IO

O Brother, Where Art Thou . . .CA, IO
Object of My Affection, The . .VR, EH
Ocean's Eleven . . . . .DI, PM
Ocean's Twelve . . . . .DI, PM
Ocean's 13 . . . . .PM, RC
October Sky . . . . .YS, MC, LW
Octopussy . . . . .CA, PM
Off the Map . . . . .ES, LW
Office Space . . . . .DI
Officer and a Gentleman, An . .VR, DI, LW
Oh God! . . . . .ES, IO
Oh Heavenly Dog . . . . .LW
Oh in Ohio . . . . .VR
Oklahoma! . . . . .CP, RL, DI
Old Boy . . . . .DH, DS, ES
Old School . . . . .IO, LW, RC
Old Yeller . . . . .DS, YS, EH
Oliver Twist . . . . .YS, DS, CP
Oliver . . . . .YS, CP
Omega Man, The . . . . .DH
Omen, The . . . . .DH
Omen 2 . . . . .DH
Omen 3 . . . . .DH
Omen 4 . . . . .DH
On Golden Pond . . . . .DS

On Her Majesty's Secret
  Service . . . . .PM, CA
On the Waterfront . . . . .PM, DI, DS
Once . . . . .CP, VR
Once Bitten . . . . .IO
Once Upon a Time in
  America . . . . .LW, PM
Once Upon a Time in
  China . . . . .PM, RC, CA
Once Upon a Time in
  the West . . . . .PM, DH
Once Were Warriors . . . . .DS, EH
One Crazy Summer . . . . .RC
One False Move . . . . .CD, PM
One Fine Day . . . . .VR
One Flew Over the
  Cuckoo's Nest . . . . .EH, LW, PM
One from the Heart . . . . .VR, CP
One Good Cop . . . . .PM, DI
One Hour Photo . . . . .DS, EH
101 Dalmations . . . . .YS, CA
One Night at McCool's . . . . . .IO, DI
Only You . . . . .VR
Open Range . . . . .LW, DH
Open Season . . . . .YS, CA
Open Water . . . . .DS, DH
Operation Dumbo Drop . . . . . .CA
Opposite of Sex, The . . . . .RL, YS
Orange County . . . . .DI, YS
Ordinary People . . . . .DS, EH
Original Sin . . . . .RL
Orlando . . . . .MC, RL
Oscar and Lucinda . . . . .VR
Oscar . . . . .DI
Osmosis Jones . . . . .IO
Other Sister, The . . . . .DS, VR
Others, The . . . . .DS, ES
Out of Africa . . . . .RL, EH
Out of Sight . . . . .RL, PM, CD
Out of the Past . . . . .CD
Out of Time . . . . .CD
Outbreak . . . . .DS, PM

Charismatic Performer: CP • Chosen Adventurer: CA •
Courageous Detective: CD • Dedicated Idealist: DI •
Destined Hunter: DH • Determined Survivor: DS •
Enlightened Healer: EH • Existential Savior: ES •
Invincible Optimist: IO • Loyal Warrior: LW •
Magical Creator: MC • Passionate Maverick: PM •
Rebellious Lover: RL • Respected Champion: RC •
Vivacious Romantic: VR • Youthful Sage: YS

Charismatic Performer: CP • Chosen Adventurer: CA •
Courageous Detective: CD • Dedicated Idealist: DI •
Destined Hunter: DH • Determined Survivor: DS •
Enlightened Healer: EH • Existential Savior: ES •
Invincible Optimist: IO • Loyal Warrior: LW •
Magical Creator: MC • Passionate Maverick: PM •
Rebellious Lover: RL • Respected Champion: RC •
Vivacious Romantic: VR • Youthful Sage: YS

Rambo III . . . . .DH, PM
Rambo IV: Pearl of the
  Cobra . . . . .DH, PM
Rambo: First Blood . . . . .DH, PM
Rambo: First Blood Part 2 . . . .DH, PM
Ran .PM
Ransom . . . . .DS, PM
Rashomon . . . . .CD
Rat Race . . . . .RC, IO
Ratatouille . . . . .MC, DY, IS
Ravenous . . . . .DH
Ray .CP, EH
Real Genius . . . . .RC, IO, YS
Real Life . . . . .IO, DI
Real Women Have Curves . . . .VR, DS
Reality Bites . . . . .DI, YS, VR
Re-Animator . . . . .DH
Reaping, The . . . . .DH, ES
Rear Window . . . . .CD
Rebecca . . . . .CD, EH, RL
Rebel Without a Cause . . . . . .PM, YS, LW, EH
Recruit, The . . . . .ES, PM
Red Balloon, The . . . . .YS, ES
Red Dawn . . . . .LW, YS, DH
Red Dragon . . . . .DH, CD
Red River . . . . .DS
Red Shoes, The . . . . .CP, DS, RL
Red Sonja . . . . .DH, CA
Red Violin, The . . . . .DS
Red .DS, EH
Reds . . . . .PM
Reefer Madness . . . . .IO, ES
Ref, The . . . . .PM, LW
Regarding Henry . . . . .DS, VR
Reign of Fire . . . . .DH, CA, LW
Reindeer Games . . . . .DH
Remains of the Day . . . . .DI, RL
Remember the Titans . . . . . . .PM, LW, RC
Renaissance . . . . .ES
Reno 911!: Miami . . . . .IO
Rent . . . . .DS, CP, EH, VR
Replacements, The . . . . .RC, LW
Repo Man . . . . .ES, DI
Repulsion . . . . .DH, ES
Requiem for a Dream . . . . . . .DS, ES
Rescue Dawn . . . . .DH
Rescuers, The . . . . .CA, YS
Rescuers Down Under, The . . . .CA, YS
Reservoir Dogs . . . . .PM, ES, LW
Return of the Jedi . . . . .YS, LW, CA
Return of the Living Dead . . . .DH

Return of the Pink Panther . . . .CD, IO
Return of the Secaucus 7 . . . . .LW, DS, DI
Revenge of the Nerds . . . . . . .RC
Revenge of the Pink Panther . . .CD, IO
Reversal of Fortune . . . . .PM, RL
Riding in Cars with Boys . . . . .YS, VR, DI
Right Stuff, The . . . . .CA, LW
Ring, The . . . . .DH
Ringu . . . . .DH
Rio Bravo . . . . .LW, DH
Rising Sun . . . . .CD
Risky Business . . . . .YS, DI
River Runs Through It, A . . . . .LW, VR, DI
River Wild, The . . . . .DH
River's Edge . . . . .DS, ES, LW
RKO 281 . . . . .DI, PM
Road House . . . . .PM
Road to Guantanamo . . . . . . .PM, DS
Road to Perdition . . . . .DH, YS, LW
Road to Wellville . . . . .IO, ES
Road Trip . . . . .IO
Road Warrior, The . . . . .PM, ES, DH
Rob Roy . . . . .PM, DH
Robe, The . . . . .PM, CA
Robin and Marian . . . . .VR, CA
Robin Hood . . . . .PM, LW
Robin Hood: Men in Tights . . .IO
RoboCop . . . . .PM, DH
Robots . . . . .YS, MC, DI
Rock n' Roll High School . . . . .YS, CP
Rock, The . . . . .CA, DH
Rock Star . . . . .CP
Rocket Man . . . . .IO
Rocketeer, The . . . . .CA
Rocky . . . . .RC, VR, DS
Rocky II . . . . .RC, DS
Rocky III . . . . .RC, DS
Rocky IV . . . . .RC, DS
Rocky V . . . . .RC
Rocky Balboa . . . . .RC
Rocky Horror Picture Show,
  The . . . : . . . . .CP, MC
Roger & Me . . . . .PM
Roll Bounce . . . . .RC
Rollerbabies . . . . .YS, ES, CA
Rollerball . . . . .RC
Roman Holiday . . . . .RL
Romancing the Stone . . . . . . .CA, VR
Rome, Open City . . . . .PM, LW, RL
Romeo and Juliet . . . . .RL, YS
Romy and Michelle's High

School Reunion . . . . .IO
Ronin . . . . .PM, DH
Rookie of the Year . . . . .YS, RC
Room with a View . . . . .VR, EH
Room With a View, A . . . . . . .VR
Rooster Cogburn . . . . .DH, LW, PM
Rope . . . . .YS, CD
Rose, The . . . . .CP
Rosemary's Baby . . . . .DH
Rounders . . . . .RC
Roxanne . . . . .CP, VR, IO
Royal Tennenbaums, The . . . . .DS, RL
Royal Velvet . . . . .DS
Ruby in Paradise . . . . .DS
Rudy . . . . .RC, LW
Rules of Attraction, The . . . . .ES, RL
Rules of Engagement . . . . . . .PM
Rules of the Game . . . . .RL, CD, DI
Rumble Fish . . . . .PM
Rumble in the Bronx . . . . . . .DH
Rumor Has It . . . . .VR
Run, Lola, Run . . . . .ES
Runaway . . . . .DH
Runaway Bride . . . . .VR
Runaway Jury . . . . .PM, CD
Runaway Train . . . . .CA
Rundown, The . . . . .DH
Running Man, The . . . . .DH
Running on Empty . . . . .YS, DS
Running with Scissors . . . . . . .YS, DS
Rush Hour . . . . .IO, LW
Rush Hour 2 . . . . .IO, LW
Rushmore . . . . .YS, RC, VR
Russian Ark . . . . .ES, PM
Ruthless People . . . . .RC

S.F.W. . . . . .PM, YS, ES
Sabrina . . . . .VR
Safe . . . . .DS
Sahara . . . . .CA
Saint, The . . . . .CA, CP, PM
Salem's Lot . . . . .DH
Salton Sea, The . . . . .DH, ES
Salvador . . . . .PM
Same Time, Next Year . . . . . . .VR
Sand Pebbles, The . . . . .PM, LW
Santa Clause, The . . . . .MC
Saturday Night Fever . . . . . . .CP, YS, VR, PM
Save the Last Dance . . . . .RL, CP, RC
Saved . . . . .YS, IO
Saving Private Ryan . . . . .LW

Saving Silverman . . . . .LW
Saw . . . . .DH
Say Anything . . . . .YS, VR
Scanner Darkly, A . . . . .ES
Scanners . . . . .ES, DH
Scarface . . . . .PM, LW
Scarlet Pimpernel, The . . . . . . .CP, PM
Scary Movie . . . . .IO, DH
Scenes from a Mall . . . . .VR, IO, RC
Scenes from a Marriage . . . . . .RL, DS
Scenes from the Class
  Struggle in Beverly Hills . . . . .DI, VR
Scent of a Woman . . . . .PM, LW
Schindler's List . . . . .DS, PM
Schizopolis . . . . .ES, DI
School Daze . . . . .YS, CP, LW
School for Scoundrels . . . . . . .LW, RC
School Ties . . . . .YS, RC, LW
Science of Sleep, The . . . . .VR, MC
Scooby Doo . . . . .CD, IO, YS
Scoop . . . . .VR, CD
Score, The . . . . .PM
Scream . . . . .DH
Screamers . . . . .DH
Scrooged . . . . .DI, IO
Sea of Love . . . . .CD, RL
Seabiscuit . . . . .RC, DS
Searchers, The . . . . .DH, PM
Searching for Bobby Fischer . . .YS, EH, RC
Secondhand Lions . . . . .YS, LW
Secret Garden, The . . . . .YS, MC
Secret Lives of Dentists, The . . .DS, LW
Secret of My Success, The . . . .DI
Secret of NIMH . . . . .CA, YS
Secret of Roan Inish, The . . . . .YS, MC
Secret Window . . . . .ES, DH
Secretary . . . . .DI, RL
Secrets and Lies . . . . .DS, EH
See No Evil, Hear No Evil . . . . .IO, LW
Sense and Sensibility . . . . .VR, EH
Serendipity . . . . .VR, MC
Serenity . . . . .YS, PM, CA

Charismatic Performer: CP • Chosen Adventurer: CA •
Courageous Detective: CD • Dedicated Idealist: DI •
Destined Hunter: DH • Determined Survivor: DS •
Enlightened Healer: EH • Existential Savior: ES •
Invincible Optimist: IO • Loyal Warrior: LW •
Magical Creator: MC • Passionate Maverick: PM •
Rebellious Lover: RL • Respected Champion: RC •
Vivacious Romantic: VR • Youthful Sage: YS

Sleeping Beauty . . . . VR, MC
Sleeping with the Enemy . . . . . DS, DH
Sleepless in Seattle . . . . VR, EH
Sleepy Hollow . . . . DH, CD
Sleuth . . . . CP, CD, RC
Sliding Doors . . . . VR, ES
Sling Blade . . . . EH, YS
Sliver . . . . RL, CD
Slums of Beverly Hills . . . . YS, DS, LW
Small Time Crooks . . . . DI, IO
Smoke Signals . . . . DS, LW
Smokey and the Bandit . . . . . . IO
Smokin' Aces . . . . DH, RC
Snake Eyes . . . . CD
Snakes on a Plane . . . . DH
Snatch . . . . PM, DI
Sneakers . . . . PM, LW
Snow Dogs . . . . CA, RC
Snow White and the
  Seven Dwarfs . . . . YS, LW, VR
So I Married an Axe
  Murderer . . . . IO, VR
So Proudly We Hail . . . . EH, LW
Solaris . . . . ES, VR
Soldier . . . . DH
Soldier's Story, A . . . . PM, DS, CD
Some Kind of Wonderful . . . . . VR, YS, RC
Some Like It Hot . . . . CP, IO
Somebody to Love . . . . VR
Someone to Watch
  Over Me . . . . RL, EH
Something to Talk About . . . . . VR
Something Wicked This
  Way Comes . . . . MC, YS, DH
Something Wild . . . . RL, EH
Something's Gotta Give . . . . . . VR, EH
Somewhere in Time . . . . RL, MC
Sommersby . . . . RL
Son of the Mask . . . . CP, MC, IO
Son of the Pink Panther . . . . . CD, IO
Song of Bernadette . . . . EH
Sophie's Choice . . . . DS, EH
Soul Food . . . . LW
Soul Man . . . . DI, CP, IO
Sound of Music, The . . . . EH, CP
Sounder . . . . YS, LW
South Pacific . . . . RL, CP
South Park: Bigger Longer &
  Uncut . . . . IO
Soylent Green . . . . ES, CA
Space Cowboys . . . . CA, LW

Spaceballs . . . . IO
Spanglish . . . . DS, YS, EH
Spanish Prisoner, The . . . . DI, CD
Spanking the Monkey . . . . RL, YS, DS
Spartacus . . . . PM, CA
Spartan . . . . PM, CD
Spawn . . . . DH
Specialist, The . . . . DH, RL
Species . . . . DH
Speed . . . . DH, CA
Spellbound (documentary) . . . RC, YS
Spellbound . . . . EH, CD, ES
Sphere . . . . ES, CA
Spider-Man . . . . CA
Spider-Man 2 . . . . CA, DH
Spider-Man 3 . . . . CA, DH
Spies Like Us . . . . IO
Spinal Tap, This Is . . . . CP, IO
Spirited Away . . . . YS, MC, CA
Spitfire Grill . . . . YS, DI
Spitfire Grill, The . . . . DS, EH
Splash . . . . VR, IO, EH
Splendor in the Grass . . . . RL
Spy Game . . . . CA, CD
Spy Kids . . . . YS, CA
Spy Who Came in From
  the Cold, The . . . . CA, PM
Spy Who Loved Me, The . . . . . PM, CA
Spy Who Shagged Me, The . . . IO
Squid and the Whale, The . . . . YS, DS, LW
St. Elmo's Fire . . . . LW, VR
Stage Door . . . . CP, VR
Stagecoach . . . . CA, LW
Stakeout . . . . CD, IO
Stalag 17 . . . . DS, CD
Stalingrad . . . . PM
Stand, The . . . . ES
Stand and Deliver . . . . EH, DI
Stand by Me . . . . LW, YS
Stanley and Iris . . . . VR, EH
Star Is Born, A . . . . CP, DS, EH
Star Trek . . . . CA, LW

Charismatic Performer: CP • **Chosen Adventurer:** CA •
Courageous Detective: CD • **Dedicated Idealist:** DI •
Destined Hunter: DH • **Determined Survivor:** DS •
Enlightened Healer: EH • **Existential Savior:** ES •
Invincible Optimist: IO • **Loyal Warrior:** LW •
Magical Creator: MC • **Passionate Maverick:** PM •
Rebellious Lover: RL • **Respected Champion:** RC •
Vivacious Romantic: VR • **Youthful Sage:** YS

Swept Away . . . . .VR
Swimming Pool . . . . .RL
Swimming to Cambodia . . . . . .DI, PM
Swimming with Sharks . . . . . .DI
Swing Time . . . . .CP, VR
Swingers . . . . .VR, LW
Swiss Family Robinson . . . . . .CA, YS, LW
Switchback . . . . .DH
Swordfish . . . . .DH
Sympathy for the Devil . . . . . .PM
Syriana . . . . .PM, CD

Tadpole . . . . .RL
Tae Guk Gi . . . . .LW
Take the Lead . . . . .CP, YS, LW
Take the Money and Run . . . . .DI
Taking Lives . . . . .DH, CD
Taking of Pelham One Two
    Three, The . . . . .PM, DH
Talented Mr. Ripley, The . . . . .MC, CP
Talk Radio . . . . .CP, DI
Talk to Her . . . . .RL, ES
Talk to Me . . . . .PM
Talladega Nights . . . . .RC, IO
Taming of the Shrew . . . . .VR, RC
Tango and Cash . . . . .PM
Tao of Steve, The . . . . .VR, PM, RC
Tape . . . . .ES, RL
Tapeheads . . . . .DI, CP
Taps . . . . .LW
Tarzan . . . . .CA, RL
Taxi Driver . . . . .DH, PM, EH
Team America World Police . . .IO
Ted Bundy . . . . .DH
Teen Witch . . . . .RC, MC
Teen Wolf . . . . .YS, RC
Teenage Mutant Ninja
    Turtles . . . . .CA
10 . . . . .VR
10 Things I Hate About You . . .YS, VR, RC
10,000 B.C. . . . . .ES, CA
Ten, The . . . . .IO
Ten Commandments, The . . . .PM, CA
Tenacious D . . . . .CP, IO
Tender Mercies . . . . .CP, DS
Tequila Sunrise . . . . .RL
Terminal, The . . . . .VR, DS
Terminator, The . . . . .DH
Terminator 2 . . . . .DH
Terminator 3 . . . . .DH
Terms of Endearment . . . . . . .DS, EH, VR

Tess . . . . .YS, RL
Tex .PM, YS
Texas Chainsaw Massacre . . . .DH
Texas Chainsaw Massacre 2 . . .DH
Texas Chainsaw Massacre 3 . . .DH
Texas Chainsaw Massacre 4 . . .DH
Texasville . . . . .DS, VR
Thank You for Smoking . . . . . .DI
That Thing You Do! . . . . .CP, YS
Thelma and Louise . . . . .PM, LW
Them . . . . .DH
There Will Be Blood . . . . .PM
There's Something About
    Mary . . . . .IO
They Call Me Bruce . . . . .IO
They Live . . . . .ES, DH
They Live by Night . . . . .PM
Thief, The . . . . .YS, EH
Thin Blue Line, The . . . . .CD, PM
Thin Man, The . . . . .CD, CP
Thin Red Line, The . . . . .LW, ES
Thing, The . . . . .DH
Third Man, The . . . . .CD
Thirteen . . . . .YS, DS
Thirteen Conversations
    About One Thing . . . . .ES, DS
Thirteen Days . . . . .PM, LW
13 Going on 30 . . . . .VR, YS
Thirteenth Floor, The . . . . . . .ES, DH
39 Steps, The . . . . .CD, DS
This Boy's Life . . . . .YS, DS, LW
This Film Is Not Yet Rated . . . .PM
This Island Earth . . . . .ES, DH
Thomas Crown Affair . . . . . . .CD, PM, RL
Those Magnificent Men in
    their Flying Machines . . . . . . .MC, RC
Three Amigos . . . . .IO, RC
Three Colors Trilogy
    (Red, White, Blue) . . . . .DS
Three Days of the Condor . . . .CD, PM
3 Godfathers . . . . .EH
300 .CA, DH

Charismatic Performer: CP • Chosen Adventurer: CA •
Courageous Detective: CD • Dedicated Idealist: DI •
Destined Hunter: DH • Determined Survivor: DS •
Enlightened Healer: EH • Existential Savior: ES •
Invincible Optimist: IO • Loyal Warrior: LW •
Magical Creator: MC • Passionate Maverick: PM •
Rebellious Lover: RL • Respected Champion: RC •
Vivacious Romantic: VR • Youthful Sage: YS

Three Kings . . . . PM, LW
Three Men and a Baby . . . . LW, VR
Throne of Blood . . . . PM, DH
Through a Glass Darkly . . . . . . DS, ES
Throw Mamma from
  the Train . . . . IO
Thumbsucker . . . . YS, DS, EH
Thunderball . . . . CA, PM
THX-1138 . . . . ES
Tideland . . . . YS, ES, CA
Tie Me Up! Tie Me Down! . . . . DS, RL
Tie That Binds, The . . . . RL, DH, DS
Tigerland . . . . LW, PM
Time Bandits . . . . CA, ES, MC
Time Code . . . . ES, DI
Time Machine, The . . . . CA, MC
Time to Kill, A . . . . PM
Timecop . . . . CA, DH
Tin Cup . . . . RC, VR, EH
Tin Drum, The . . . . DS, PM
Titan A.E. . . . . YS, CA
Titanic . . . . RL, CA
Titus . . . . PM
To Be or Not to Be . . . . IO
To Catch a Thief . . . . CD
To Die For . . . . CP, RL
To Have and Have Not . . . . PM, RL
To Kill a Mockingbird . . . . PM, YS
To Live and Die in L.A. . . . . . . CD, PM
To Live . . . . DI
Tokyo Godfathers . . . . LW
Tokyo Story . . . . DS
Tom & Viv . . . . RL, CP
Tom Jones . . . . CP, VR
Tomb Raider . . . . CA
Tombstone . . . . DH, PM
Tommy . . . . DS, MC, CP
Tommy Boy . . . . IO, DI, LW
Tootsie . . . . CP, VR
Top Gun . . . . PM, CA
Top Secret . . . . IO
Topsy Turvy . . . . CP
Tora! Tora! Tora! . . . . LW
Tortilla Soup . . . . LW, DS
Total Recall . . . . DH, CA, ES
Touch of Evil . . . . CD, PM
Towering Inferno, The . . . . DS, PM, LW
Toxic Avenger, The . . . . DH, IO
Toy, The . . . . LW, YS, DI, RC
Toy Soldiers . . . . YS, LW, DH
Toy Story . . . . CA, LW

Trading Places . . . . RC, DI
Traffic . . . . CD, DS
Training Day . . . . PM
Trainspotting . . . . ES
Trancers . . . . DH, ES
Transamerica . . . . DS, CP
Transformers . . . . CA
Transporter, The . . . . DH
Trash . . . . ES
Treasure of the Sierra
  Madre, The . . . . DH, LW
Treasure Planet . . . . CA, YS
Tremors . . . . DH
Triplets of Belleville . . . . ES, CP
Tristan and Isolde . . . . RL, YS
Tristram Shandy . . . . IO, CP
Tron . . . . ES, CA, MC
Trouble with Harry, The . . . . . . ES
Troy . . . . CA, DH
True Crime . . . . CD, DH
True Grit . . . . PM, DH
True Lies . . . . DH, CA
True Romance . . . . RL, PM
True Stories . . . . ES, DI
Truly Madly Deeply . . . . RL, DS, EH
Truman Show, The . . . . ES, DI
Trust . . . . DS, VR
Trust the Man . . . . VR
Truth about Cats and
  Dogs, The . . . . VR, CP
Tsotsi . . . . YS, LW, EH, DS
Tuck Everlasting . . . . MC, YS
Tucker . . . . PM, MC
Tully . . . . DS
Turner and Hooch . . . . LW
Tuxedo, The . . . . CA, IO
12 Angry Men . . . . CD, DI, PM
12 Monkeys . . . . ES, EH
Twelve O'clock High . . . . PM, DH
Twentieth Century . . . . CP, RC
28 Days . . . . DS, EH
28 Days Later . . . . DH
28-Up . . . . DS
28 Weeks Later . . . . DH
25th Hour . . . . PM, LW, DS
2046 . . . . ES, RL
24 Hour Party People . . . . DI, PM
21 Grams . . . . DS, RL, ES, EH
2010 . . . . ES
20,000 Leagues Under the Sea . CA
Twilight Zone: The Movie . . . . ES

Twins . . . . .LW
Twister . . . . .CA
Two Days in the Valley . . . . . .PM, DI
Two for the Money . . . . .LW, RC
Two for the Road . . . . .VR
200 Cigarettes . . . . .VR
Two Jakes, The . . . . .CD
Two-Lane Blacktop . . . . .PM, YS
2001: A Space Odyssey . . . . . .ES
Two Weeks Notice . . . . .VR

U-571 . . . . .LW
U Turn . . . . .ES, RL, DH
U.S. Vs. John Lennon, The . . .PM, CP
UHF . . . . .DI, IO, RC
Ulee's Gold . . . . .DS
Umberto D. . . . . .DS, LW
Umbrellas of Cherbourg, The . .VR, CP
Un Chien Andalou . . . . .ES
Unbearable Lightness of
   Being, The . . . . .VR, DS
Unbelievable Truth, The . . . . .DI, VR
Unbreakable . . . . .ES, DH
Uncle Buck . . . . .YS, IO, DI
Under Siege . . . . .DH
Under the Tuscan Sun . . . . . . .VR, DS, EH
Undercover Brother . . . . .IO
Underdog . . . . .RC, CA
Unfaithful . . . . .RL
Unfaithfully Yours . . . . .RL
Unfinished Life, An . . . . .DS, VR
Unforgiven . . . . .DH, PM
United 93 . . . . .DS, DH
United States of Leland . . . . . .DS, CD, RL
Unlawful Entry . . . . .DH
Unmarried Woman, An . . . . . .DS
Unsinkable Molly
   Brown, The . . . . .VR, CP
Untamed Heart . . . . .VR, EH
Untouchables, The . . . . .LW, DH
Up Close and Personal . . . . . . .VR, DI
Up in Smoke . . . . .IO
Upside of Anger, The . . . . .RL
Uptown Girls . . . . .YS, VR
Urban Cowboy . . . . .VR, PM
Urban Legend . . . . .DH
Used Cars . . . . .DI
Used Guys . . . . .IO, RC
Usual Suspects, The . . . . .CD, PM

V for Vendetta . . . . .PM, DI

Valley Girl . . . . .VR
Valley of the Dolls . . . . .DS, CP
Vampire Hunter D . . . . .DH
Van Helsing . . . . .DH, CA
Van Wilder . . . . .RC, IO, LW
Vanilla Sky . . . . .ES, DI
Vanishing, The . . . . .CD, DH, ES
Vanity Fair . . . . .RL
Varsity Blues . . . . .RC, LW
Vegas Vacation . . . . .DI, LW, IO
Verdict, The . . . . .PM, CD
Veronica Guerin . . . . .PM
Vertigo . . . . .CD, RL
Very Bad Things . . . . .DH, IO
Very Long Engagement, A . . . .CA, VR
Vibes . . . . .IO, VR
Vice Verca . . . . .YS, LW
Victor Victoria . . . . .CP, VR
Videodrome . . . . .ES, DH
View to a Kill, A . . . . .PM, CA
Village of the Damned . . . . . . .DH
Village, The . . . . .CA, DS
Virgin Spring, The . . . . .DS, DH
Virgin Suicides, The . . . . .DS, YS
Volver . . . . .DS

Wag the Dog . . . . .PM, CP
Wages of Fear . . . . .LW
Wait Until Dark . . . . .DH, DS
Waiting . . . . .DI, IO
Waiting for Guffman . . . . .CP, IO
Waiting to Exhale . . . . .VR, LW
Waking Life . . . . .ES
Waking the Dead . . . . .DI
Waking Up in Reno . . . . .LW, VR
Walk in the Clouds, A . . . . . . .RL, DS
Walk on the Moon, A . . . . . . .RL
Walk on Water . . . . .RL
Walk the Line . . . . .CP, EH, VR
Walk to Remember, A . . . . . . .VR, DS, EH
Walkabout . . . . .YS, DS
Walking and Talking . . . . .VR, DS

Charismatic Performer: CP · **Chosen Adventurer:** CA ·
Courageous Detective: CD · **Dedicated Idealist:** DI ·
Destined Hunter: DH · **Determined Survivor:** DS ·
Enlightened Healer: EH · **Existential Savior:** ES ·
Invincible Optimist: IO · **Loyal Warrior:** LW ·
Magical Creator: MC · **Passionate Maverick:** PM ·
Rebellious Lover: RL · **Respected Champion:** RC ·
Vivacious Romantic: VR · **Youthful Sage:** YS

Charismatic Performer: CP • Chosen Adventurer: CA •
Courageous Detective: CD • Dedicated Idealist: DI •
Destined Hunter: DH • Determined Survivor: DS •
Enlightened Healer: EH • Existential Savior: ES •
Invincible Optimist: IO • Loyal Warrior: LW •
Magical Creator: MC • Passionate Maverick: PM •
Rebellious Lover: RL • Respected Champion: RC •
Vivacious Romantic: VR • Youthful Sage: YS

About the Authors ★★★★★★★★★★★★★★★★★★★★★★★★★

Risa Williams has a master's degree in psychology from Antioch University, and she specializes in cognitive behavioral therapy. She also holds a master's degree in dramatic writing from New York University, and she has had plays produced at the Kennedy Center (Washington, D.C.) and the Old Globe Theater (San Diego). She lives in Los Angeles.

Ezra Werb earned a bachelor's degree in film studies and English/American Literature from Brandeis University. He lives in Los Angeles, where he works as a behaviorist for an autistic child when he is not writing screenplays. Both he and Risa have spent countless hours analyzing thousands of films.

Acknowledgments ★★★★★★★★★★★★★★★★★★★★★★★★★

A huge thanks to our literary agent, Jacqueline Hackett, Melissa Wagner at Quirk Books, Eric Hamlin, Kathy Theodore, Gregory Dicum, Ryan Golembeske, Jane Maschka, Timothy Williams, Jill Soloway, Joseph Campbell (our inspiration), and everyone who donated money and/or visited Cinescopes.com and submitted their lists. Warm thanks to our families, significant others, and friends for their continual love and support.